RISE AGAIN

VOLUME TWO FROM THE COLLECTION *ENTHUSIASM UNKNOWN TO MANKIND*

RISE AGAIN

JIM HARBAUGH | DAVID TURNLEY

Special thanks to Sarah Harbaugh, Jackie Harbaugh, and the entire Harbaugh and Feuerborn families; Charlie and Dawson, and the entire Turnley family; Warde Manuel, Doug Gnodtke, and the Michigan Athletic Department; President Mark Schlissel, Dean Guna Nadarajan, Director Jon Wells, and the Faculties of The University of Michigan Penny W. Stamps School of Art and Design, and the Residential College; David Ablauf; Nick Keebaugh; Scott Hirth and the MDen; Anne Feighan, Dan Arment, and the Michigan Alumni Association; Leica Camera; Nancy Wolff; Jon Denniston; Patrick Young; and all past, present and future Coaches and Players of The University of Michigan Football Team. A very special thanks to Rachel Turnley, J.T. Rogan, Elizabeth O'Keefe, Coach Jack Harbaugh, and Coach Jim Harbaugh.

ISBN: 978-0-692-88994-7

Designed by Elizabeth O'Keefe

10 9 8 7 6 5 4 3 2 1

Printed in China

Printed and bound by Oceanic Graphic International

Enthusiasm Productions

Enthusiasmunknowntomankind.com

A DECLARATION
OF COURAGE AND TRUE LEADERSHIP

Coach Schembechler's famous saying, "The Team, The Team, The Team" still helps put life into perspective today.

We are all associated with many teams. Our family is a team, our university is a team, our country is a team as well as this great world that we live in. We always owe it to our teammates to do as much as possible to benefit our team.

When the powers that be did not permit Michigan Football player Willis Ward to play in the 1934 football game here at Michigan Stadium against Georgia tech, they failed to stand up for civil rights, equality and social justice. We have since learned that this type of injustice should not be tolerated and it should never take place again.

Colin Kaepernick was alone in his early protests last year when he boldly and courageously confronted perceived inequalities in our social-justice system by refusing to stand for the national anthem. At times in our nation's history, we have been all too quick to judge and oppose our fellow Americans for exercising their First Amendment right to address things they believe unjust.

Rather than besmirch their character, we must celebrate their act. For we cannot pioneer and invent if we are fearful of deviating from the norm, damaging our public perception or—most important—harming our own personal interests.

I thank Colin Kaepernick for all he has contributed to the game of football as an outstanding player and trusted teammate. I also applaud Colin for the courage he has demonstrated in exercising his guaranteed right of Free Speech.

His willingness to take a position at personal cost is now part of our American story. How lucky for us all and for our country to have among our citizens someone as remarkable as Colin Kaepernick.

True leadership is standing up on behalf of the marginalized to always do what is right.

We are grateful to all those who have fought, and who continue to fight, for social justice at our university, in our country and around the world.

Jim Harbaugh

It has been an honor and pleasure to be associated with David Turnley over these past two and a half years. He is a true professional, a Pulitzer Prize Winning Photographer, and a trusted friend and ally of The University of Michigan Football Team. In *Rise Again*, David has produced another outstanding photo history, this one about our 2016/17 U of M football season.

David and I are also proud in this book to collaborate with my father, Jack Harbaugh. A National Championship Winning Coach, who has coached over 40 years, he is the wisest, most motivational man, and the best father anyone could ever wish for. He is also an extraordinary storyteller. My father and I are proud to contribute to this book, these 100 Harbaugh family motivational quotes that we have collected over all these years and that serve for us as inspiration. This collection includes family mantras along with quotes from leaders who are respected by our family. These leaders include Bo Schembechler, Winston Churchill, Ralph Waldo Emerson, George Patton and others. Our wish is that with David's outstanding photography, the selected quotes, philosophies, and ideals of the Harbaugh family will be an added bonus for you. I hope you will enjoy Rise Again and you will support our 2017 University of Michigan Football Team.

Go Blue!

JIM HARBAUGH

PHOTOGRAPHS

The priorities I have in my life are Faith, then Family, then Football.
—Jack Harbaugh

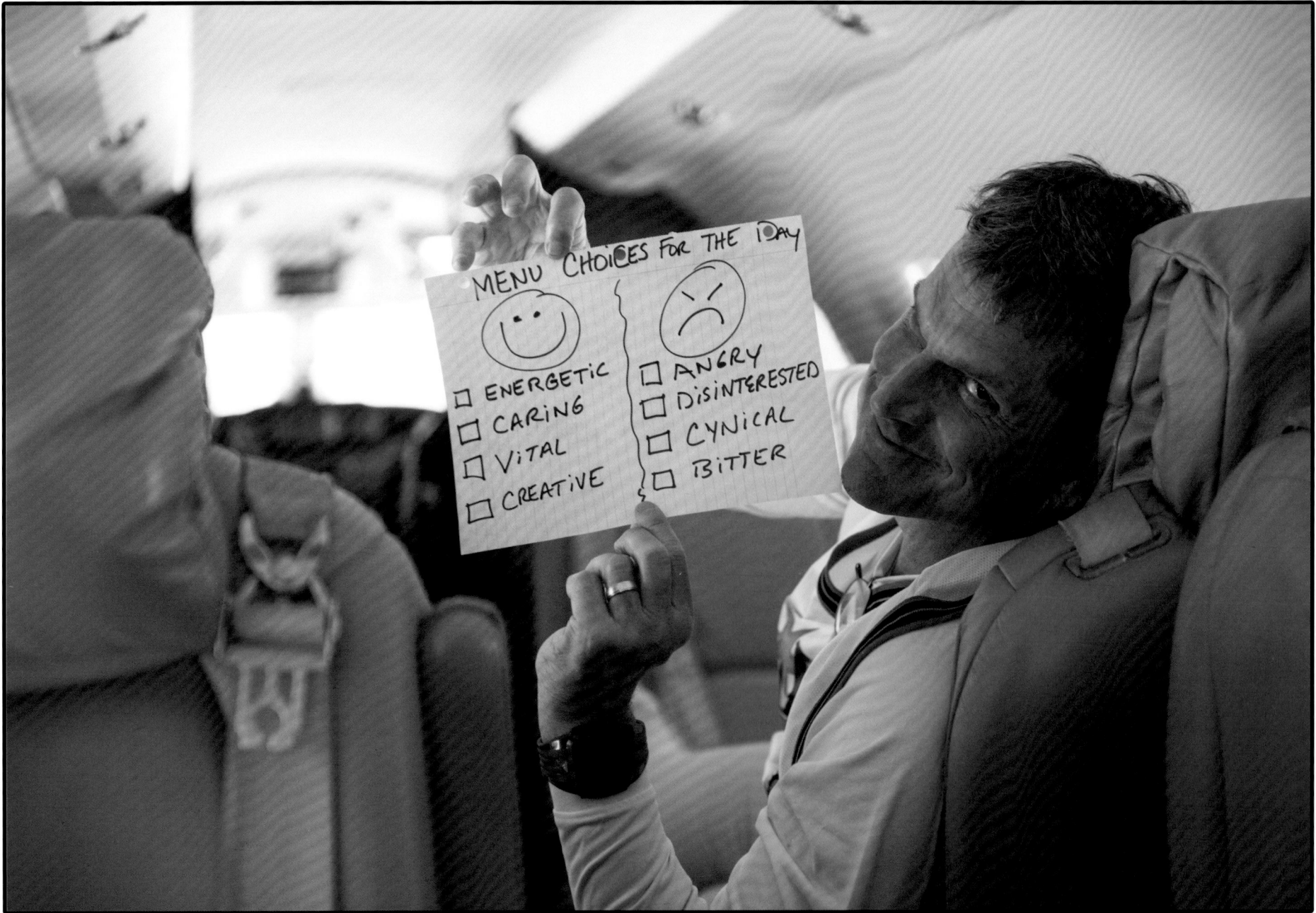

2   To me no coach in America asks a man to make a sacrifice. He requests the opposite, live clean, come clean, think clean. Stop doing things that destroy you mentally, physically, and morally and begin doing things that make you keener, finer, and more competent.

—Fielding H. Yost

Attack this day with an enthusiasm unknown to mankind.
—Jack Harbaugh

Those who stay will be champions!
—Bo Schembechler

Those who work hard will stay!
—Jim Harbaugh

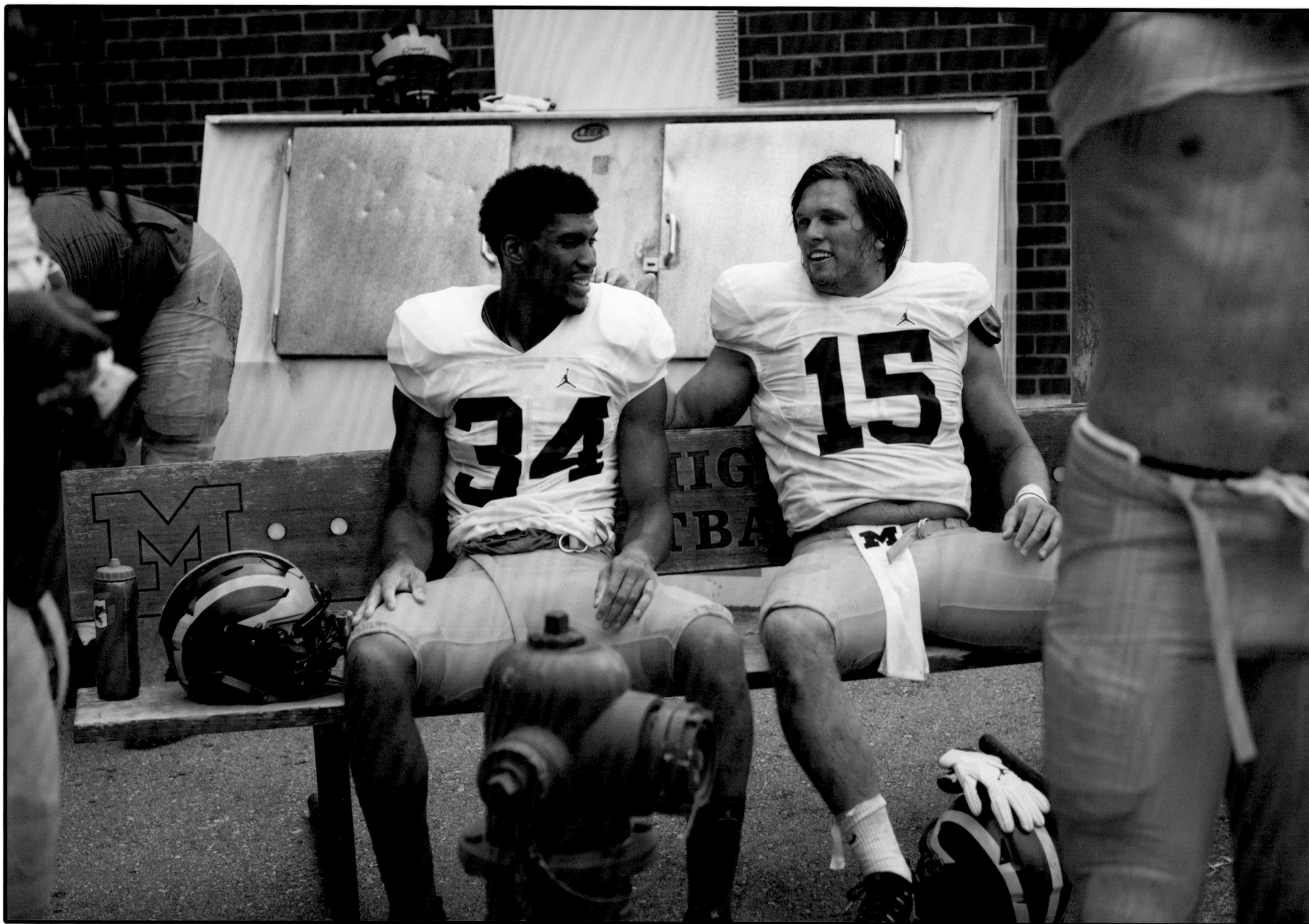

People often think that there is a General who makes all the difference, but I reject that.
It's a team effort. It's the power of the wedge.
—Jim Harbaugh

14   Whatever you vividly imagine, ardently believe, and enthusiastically act upon will inevitably come to pass.
—Paul J Meyer, through Bo Schembechler

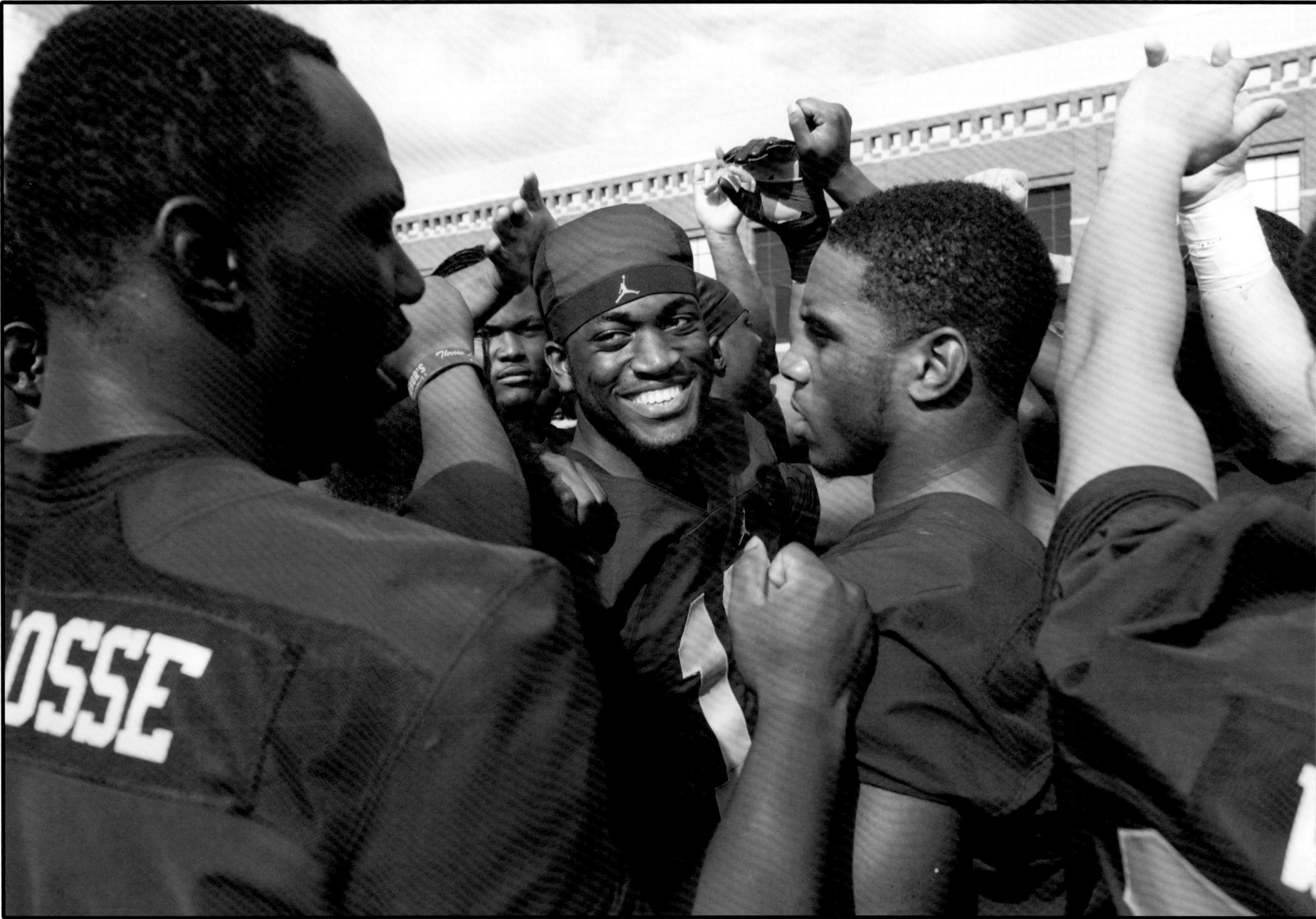

Why Play Football?
There's no other place where a young man is held to a higher standard. Football is hard, it's tough,
it demands discipline, it teaches obedience, it builds character. Football is a metaphor for life.
—John Harbaugh

18

There is a destiny that makes us brothers; None goes his way alone.
All that we send into the lives of others comes back into our own.
—Edwin Markham

The successful coach is the one who sets the trend, not the one who follows it.
—Bear Bryant

Four Ways I Could Cheat My Players: Do for them what they can do for themselves. • Allow them to get by on less than their best effort. • Allow them to believe their athletic talent is the only education they will need. • Allow them to believe that football makes them privileged.
—Woody Hayes

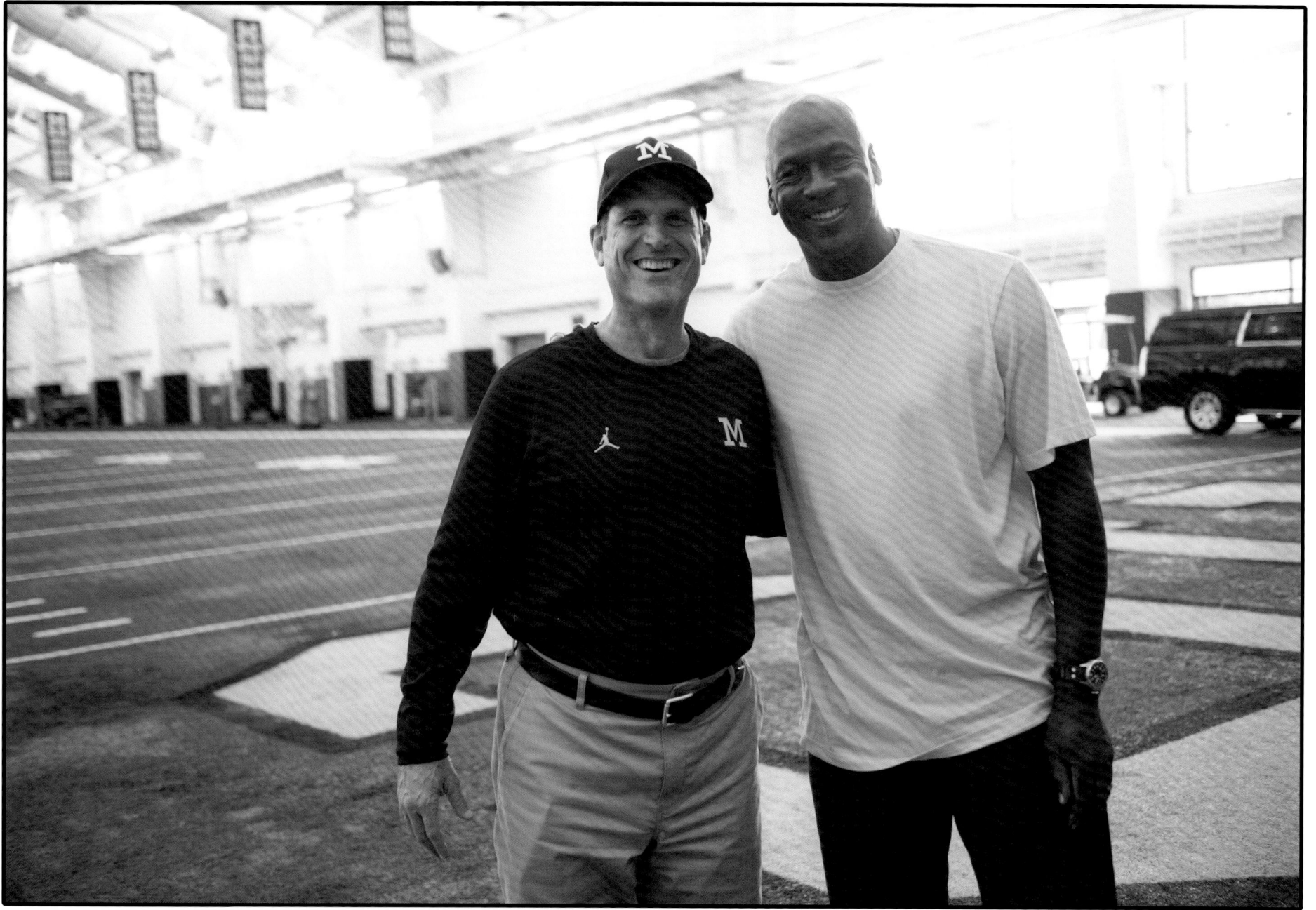

Football is the last bastion of hope for developing toughness in the American male.
—Jim Harbaugh

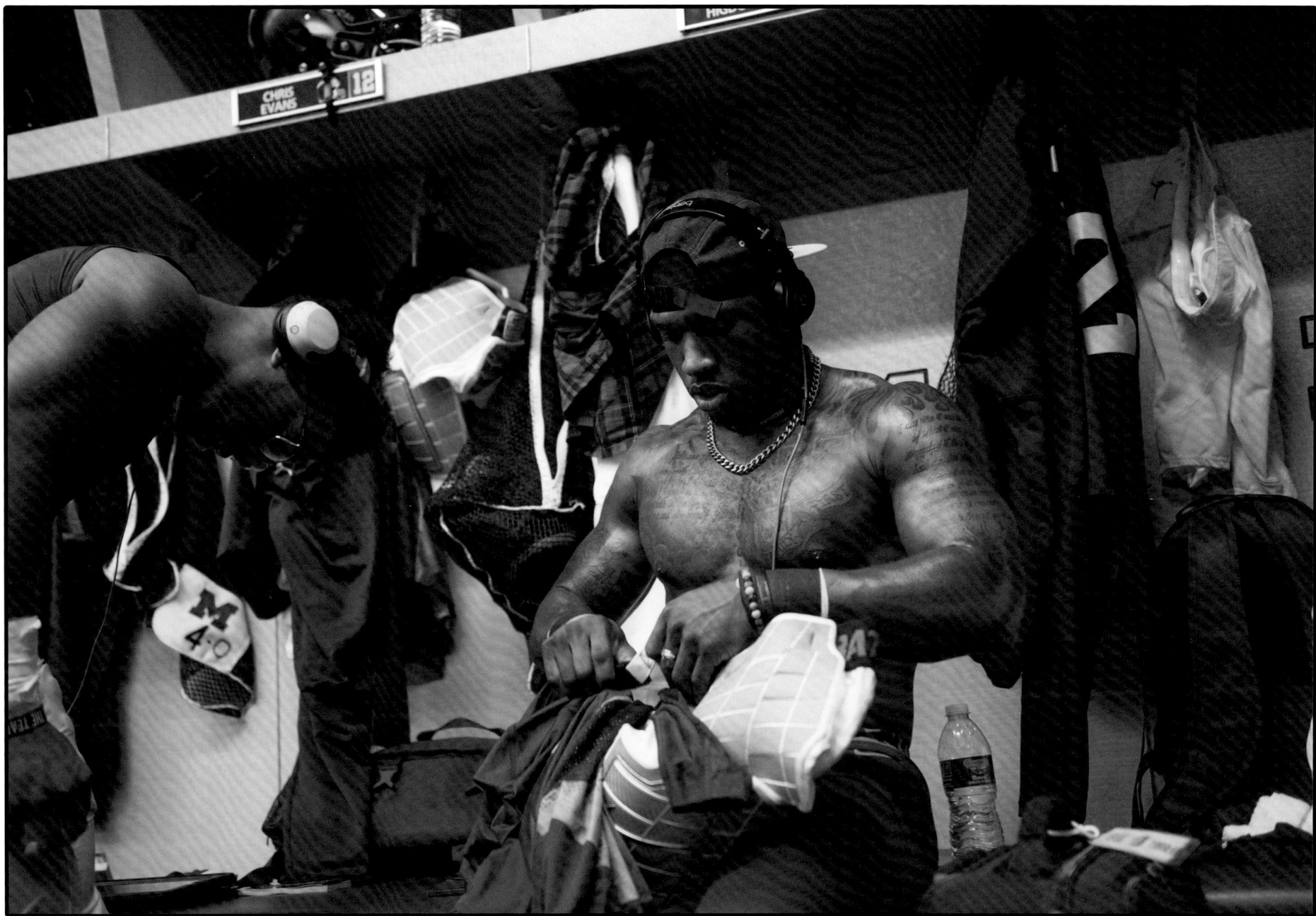

Nothing in this world can take the place of persistence. Talent will not; nothing is more common than unsuccessful men with talent. Genius will not; unrewarded genius is almost a proverb. Education will not; the world is full of educated derelicts. Persistence and determination alone are omnipotent.

—Calvin Coolidge

Who has it better than us?
Nooobody
—Jack Harbaugh

42   Tact is the ability to tell someone to go to hell in such a way that they will enjoy the trip.
—Winston Churchill

I think my brother is a great coach because he's Jim. He's a good decision maker. He makes good judgments. He's got a vision. He has a picture of what he wants it to look like. He's not worried about what other people think. He's not afraid to be himself. He is a good person and he cares about people. He wants them to do well so they can shine, not for any other reason than they can be their very best.

—John Harbaugh

Discipline is not a light switch. Discipline is a way of life.
—John Harbaugh

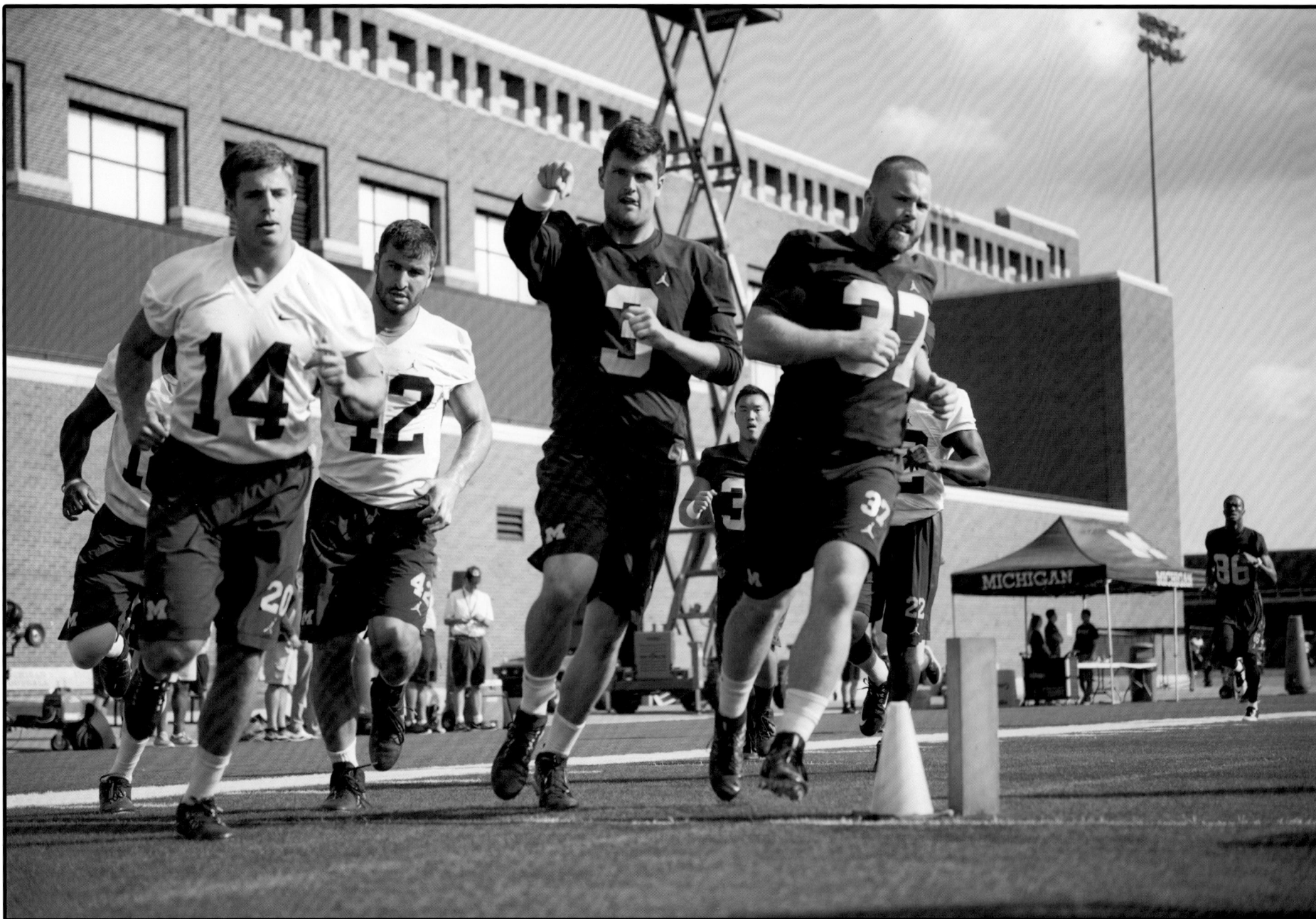

Learn from the mistakes of others. You can't live long enough to make them all yourself.
—Eleanor Roosevelt

Agents of change are never the most popular people in the room, nor should they be.
—Todd Anson

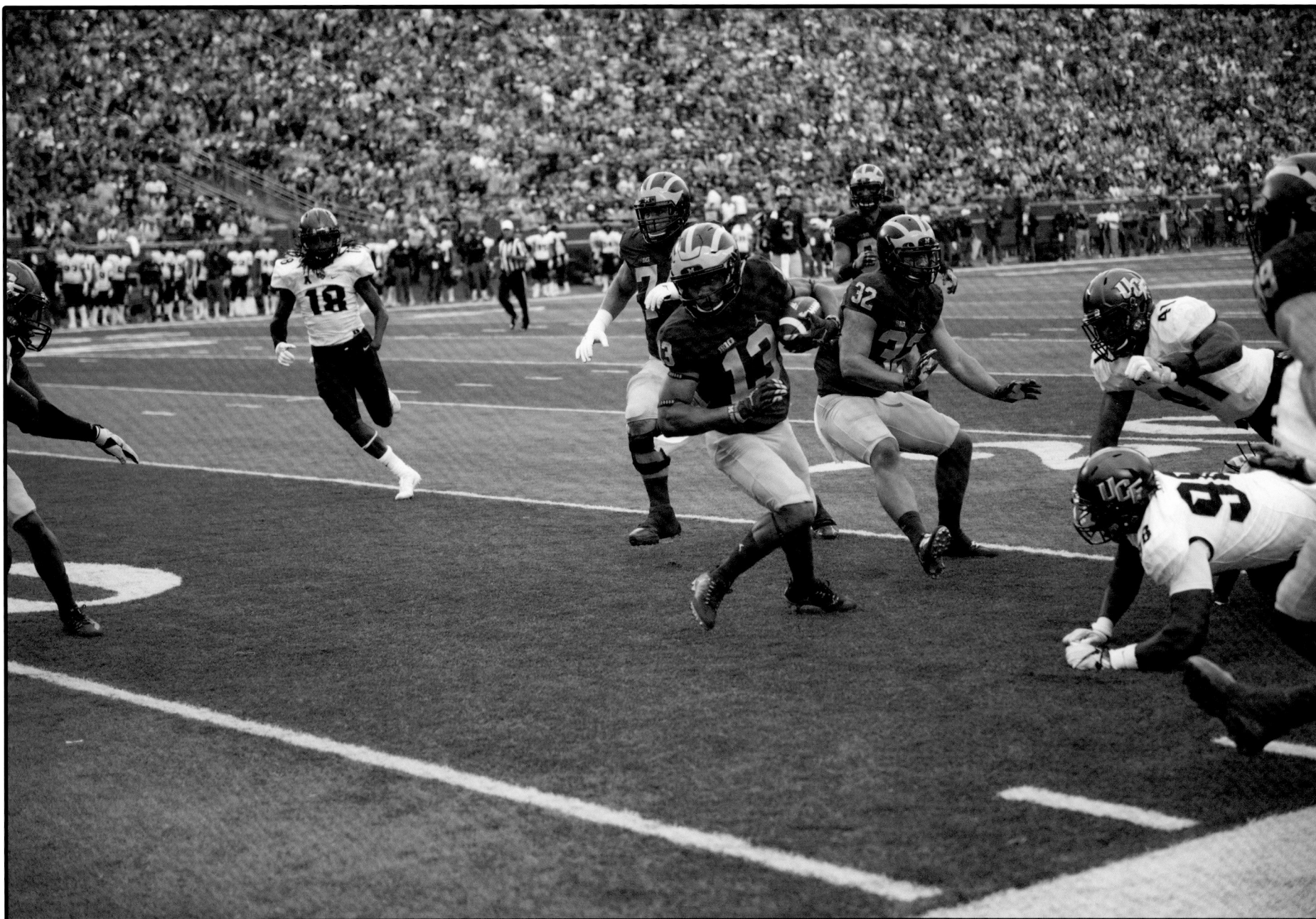

Never lie, never cheat, never steal. Don't make excuses, don't point fingers, don't pout.
—Bill Harbaugh

I wasn't born to follow and I'm not sure I was born to lead, but what I am sure is
that I was born to fight my way through this day and win.
—Jim Harbaugh

If everyone is thinking alike, then somebody isn't thinking.
—George Patton

The higher you make the risk out of proportion to the gain, the more people are likely to sit out the hand.
—Jim Rockford

You are with whom you associate.

—Jack Harbaugh

Be with wise men and you become wise. Be with evil men and you become evil.
—Proverbs 13:20

Tradition is something you can't bottle. You can't buy it at the corner store. But it is there to sustain you when you need it most. I've called upon it time and time again and so have countless other Michigan athletes and coaches. There is nothing like it. I hope it never dies.

—Fritz Crisler

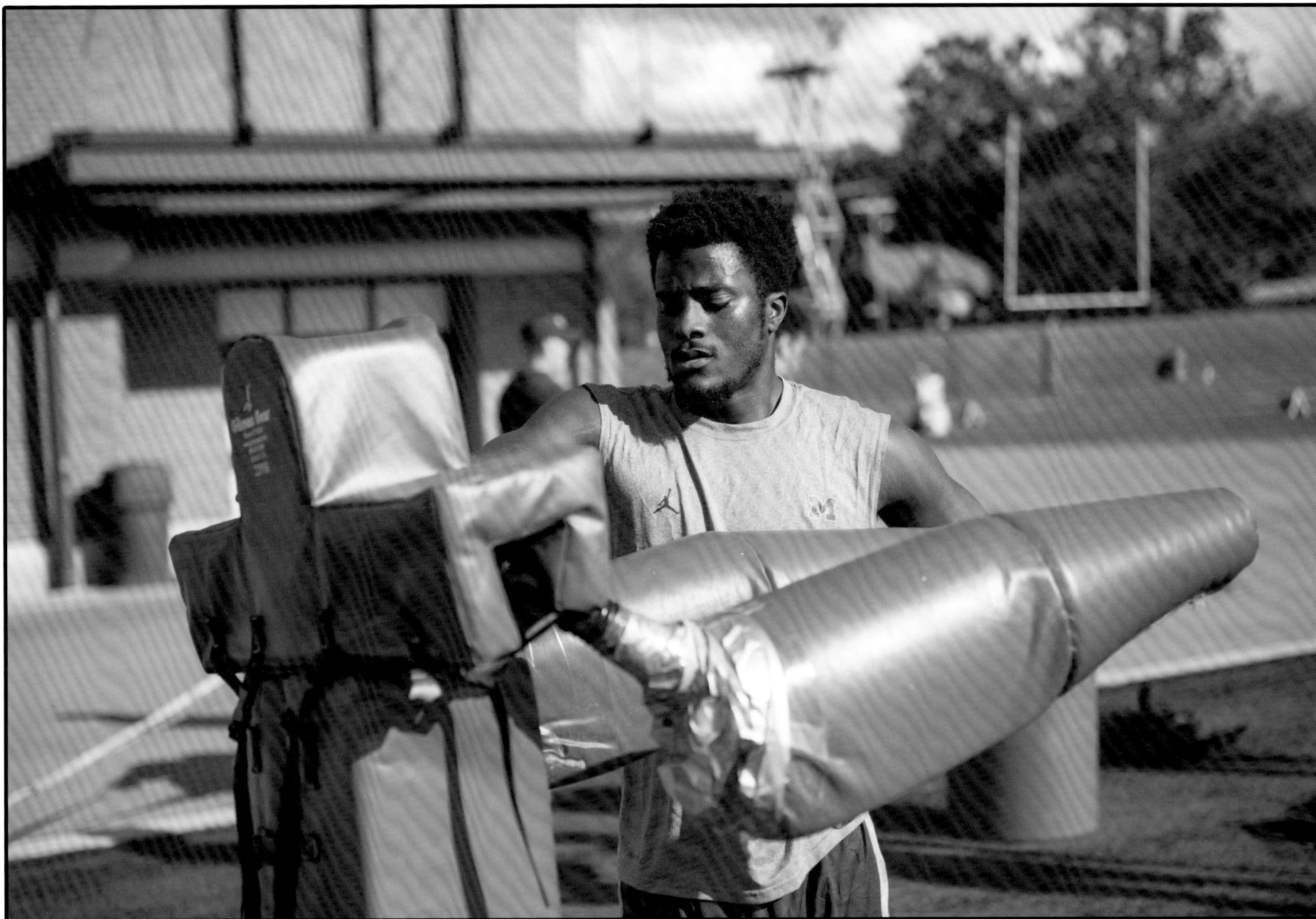

Players that learn the value of commitment, teamwork and sacrifice are the ones that make their teams great.
—Tom Crean

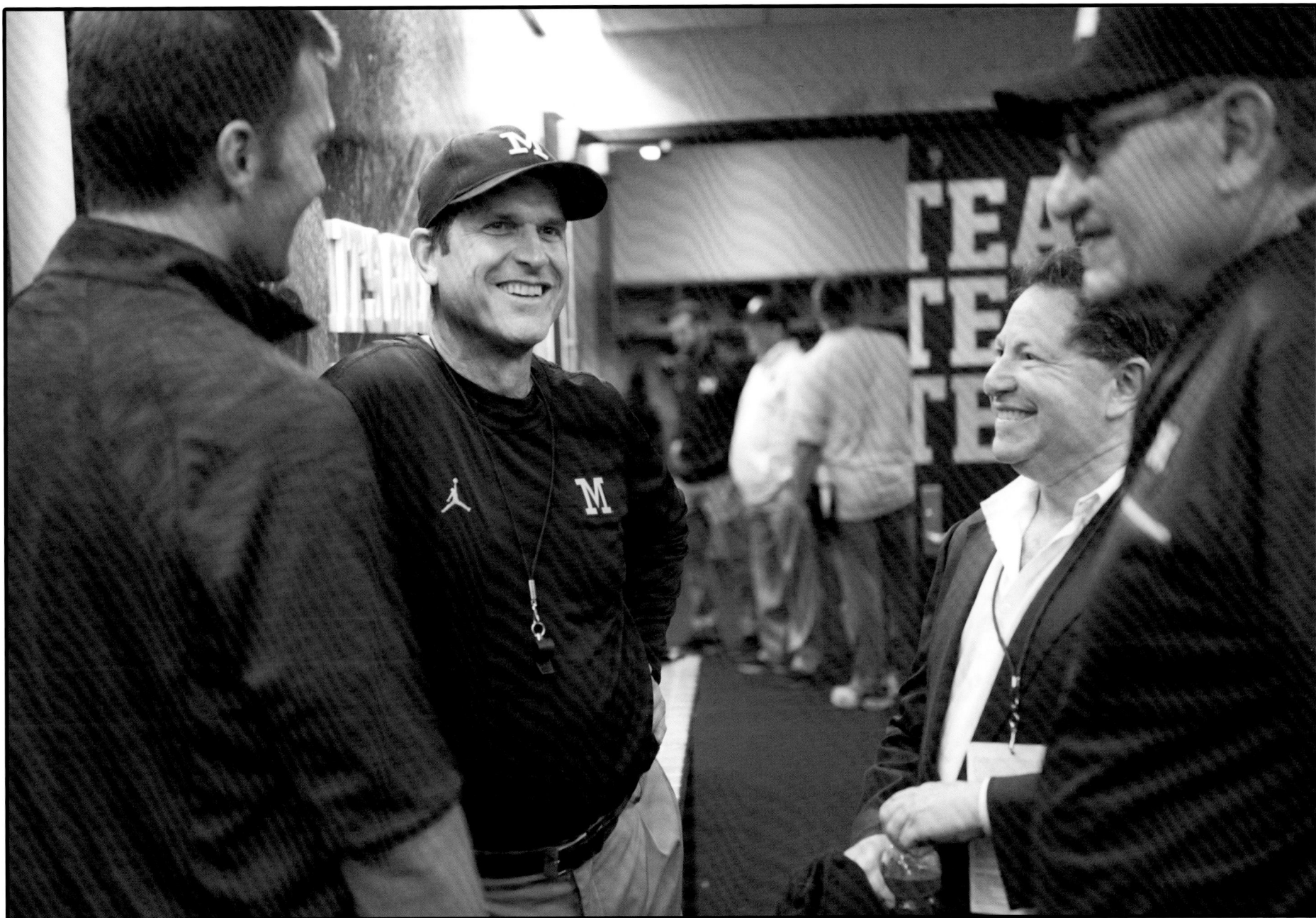

Do right. Do your best. Treat others as you want to be treated.
—Lou Holtz

In this world, you can choose to be positive or you can choose to be negative. You can choose to see things through a set of eyes that sees good, or you can choose to see things in life that aren't so good. The decision rests with you.

—Jack Harbaugh

We support no cause foreign or domestic, other than The University of Michigan Football Team.
—Jim Harbaugh

What is discipline?
Knowing what has to be done.
When it has to be done. • Doing it to the best of your God given ability. • Every day of your life.
—Bobby Knight

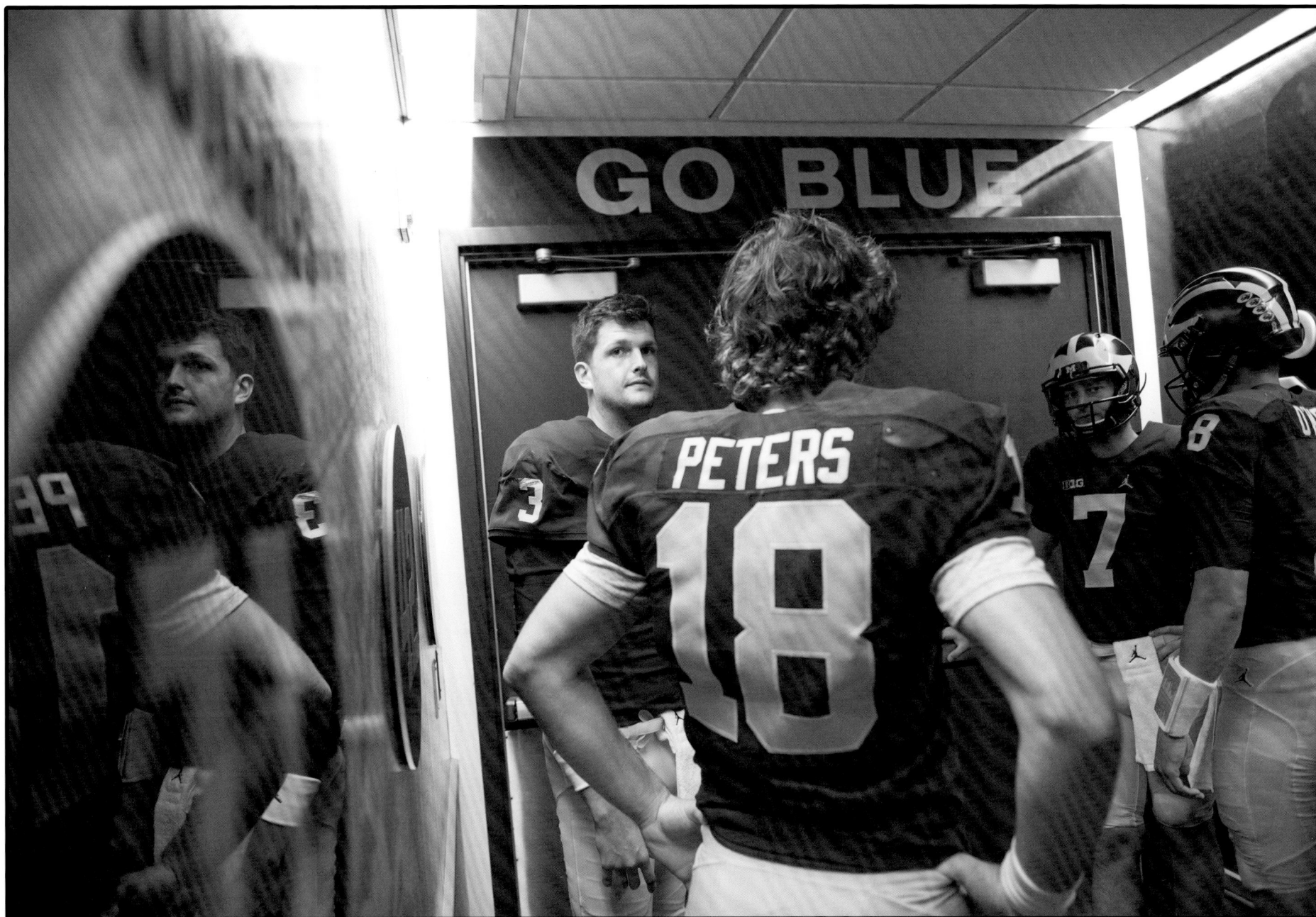

Talent determines what you can do, motivation determines how hard you will work,
attitude determines how well you will do it.
—Lou Holtz

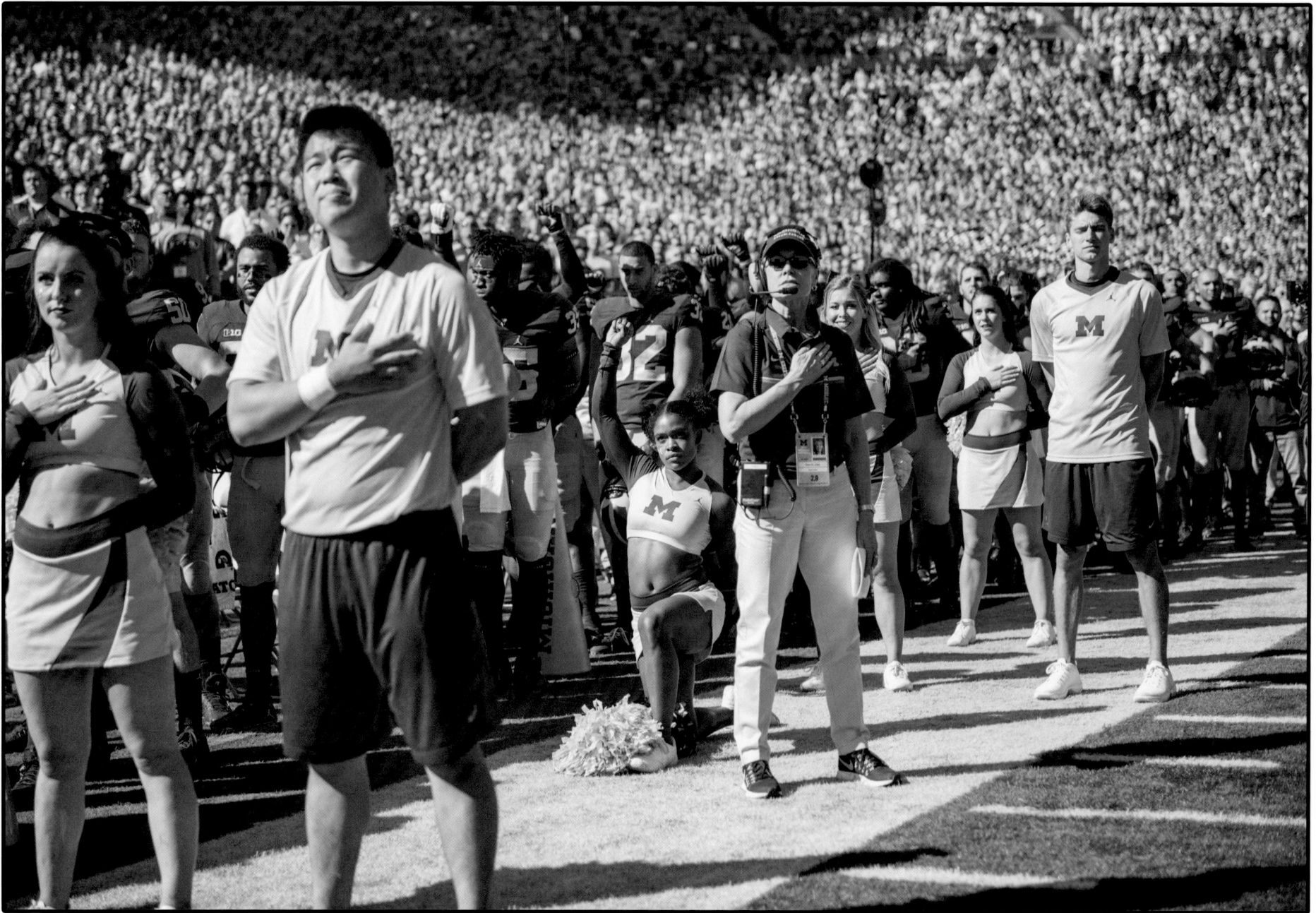

Our dad made everything competitive for me and my brother. It was always a World Championship, a National Championship, a Big 10 Championship. A championship was always at stake in everything we did.
—John Harbaugh

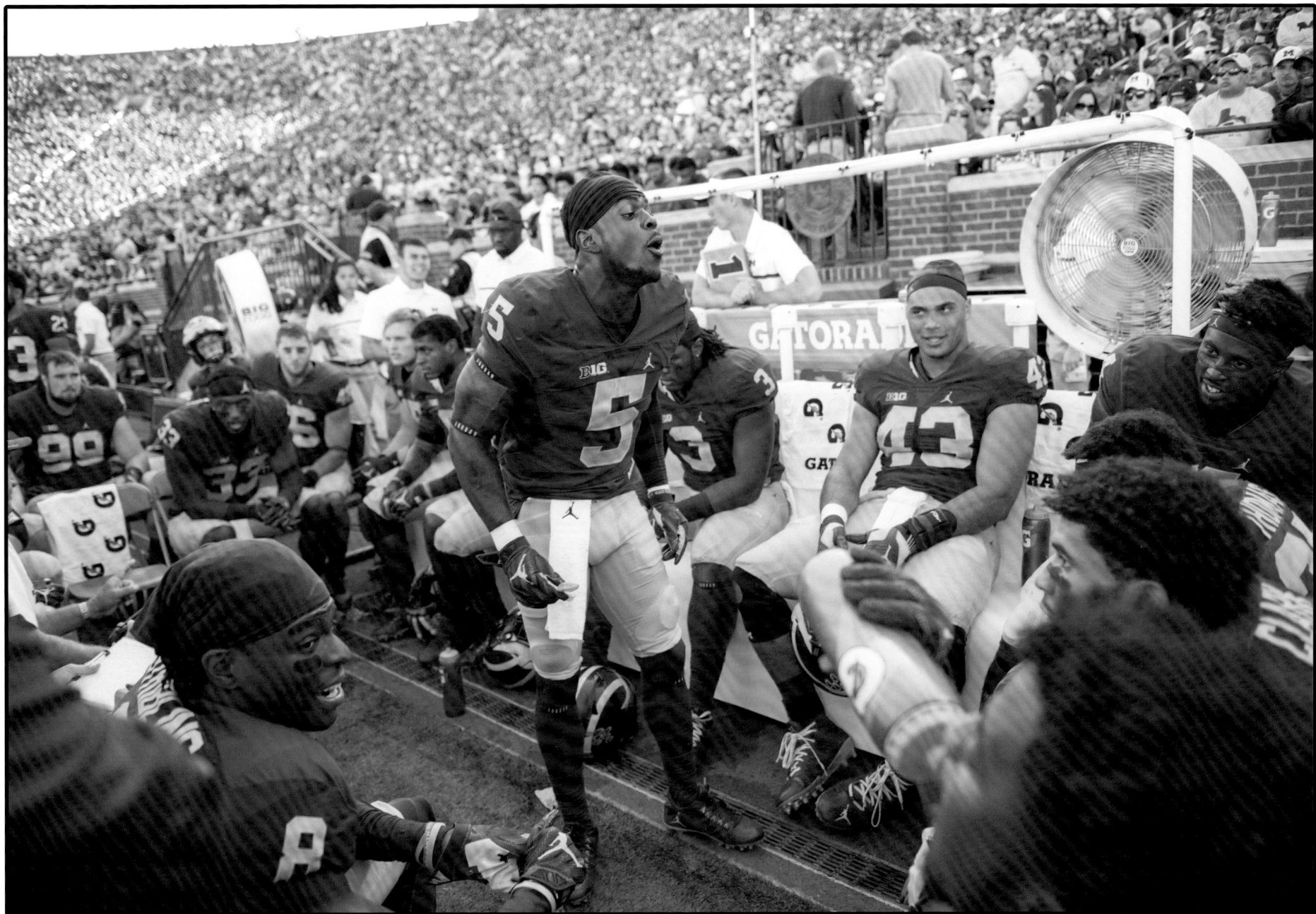

You've got to be yourself, and if you're not, you're a phony. It comes shining through for the world to see.
—Jack Harbaugh

102   Fierce, focused competition keys championships. Spirited competition will determine reps, playing time, and starting positions. This is the meritocracy on which a Michigan Team is built.
—Jim Harbaugh

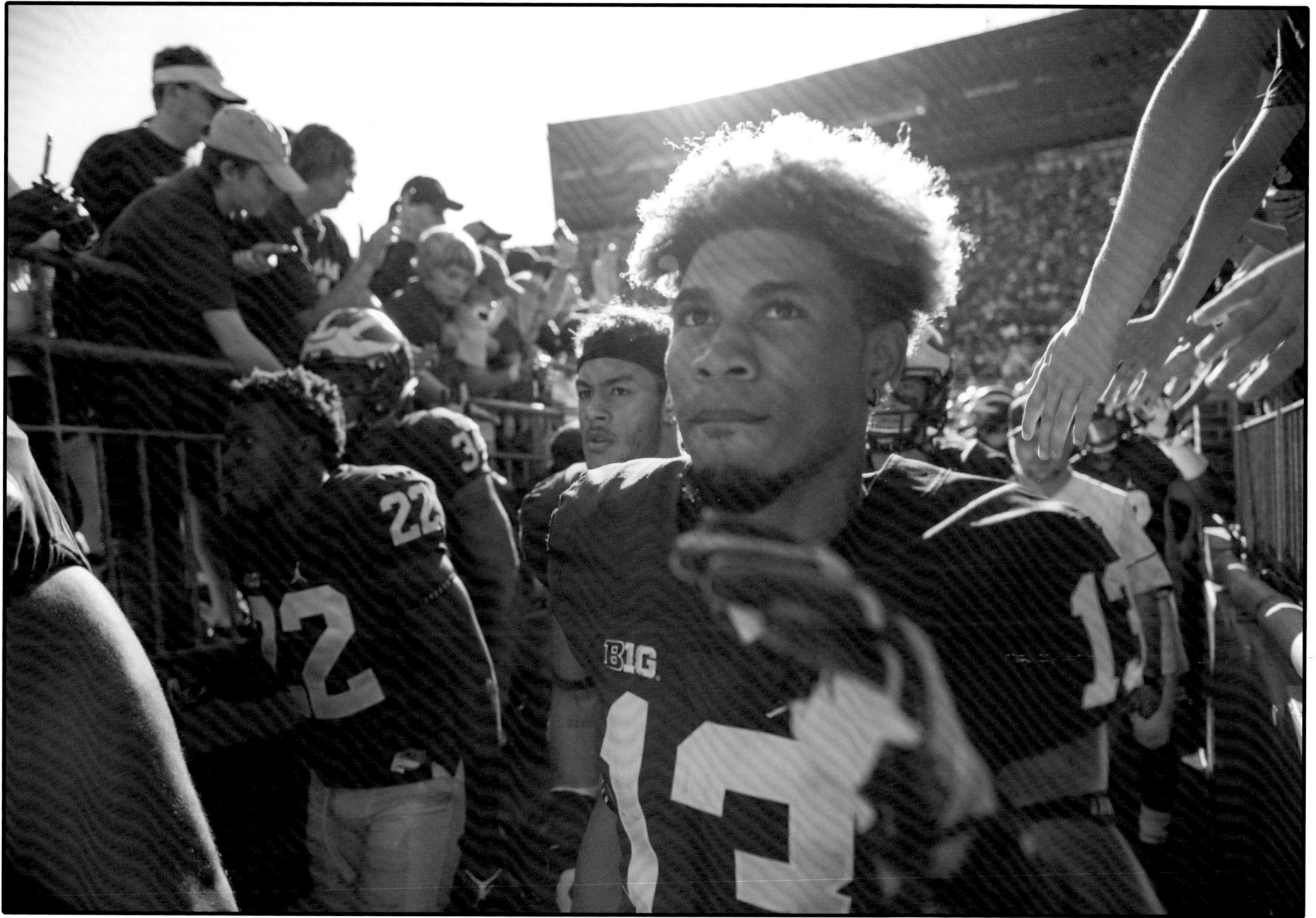

Injuries! The Doctor tells me I have 6 months of recovery; I cut that in half. He tells me I have 3 months recovery; I cut that in half. He tells me I have a 4 week recovery; I cut that in half. He tells me I have a 6 day recovery; I cut that in half. Does that make me a better man than the next guy? Yes, yes it does.

—Jim Harbaugh

"Fight on, my men," Sir Andrew said, "A little of me wounded but not yet slain;
I'll lie down and bleed a while, Then I'll rise to fight again."
—Sir Andrew Barton

Better today than yesterday, better tomorrow than today.
—Jim Harbaugh

You need to overcome the tug of people against you as you reach for high goals.
—George Patton

It's not what we have in life, but who we have in our life that matters.
—J.M. Laurence, through Joani Crean

124   Finish each day and be done with it. You have done what you could. Some blunders and absurdities no doubt, have crept in; forget them as soon as you can. Tomorrow is a new day. You shall begin it serenely and with too high a spirit to be encumbered with your old nonsense.

—Ralph Waldo Emerson

If you must fight in the North Atlantic, you must train in the North Atlantic.
—Admiral Nimitz, through Bo Schembechler

Five prerequisites to winning a National Championship:
A supportive administration • A great staff and great players
A vision, a plan and great patience • Hard work • Great team/morale
—Jim Harbaugh

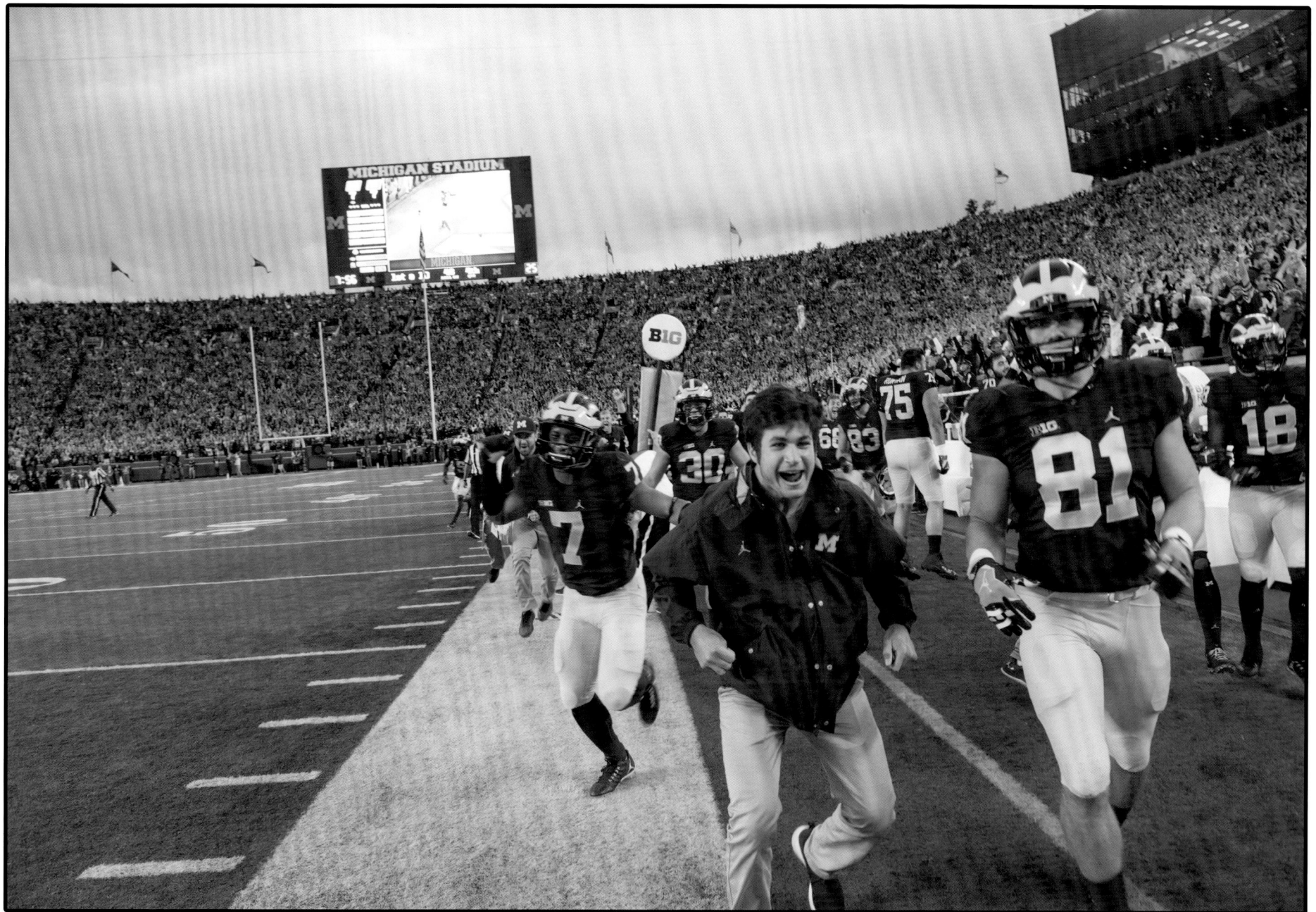

Enthusiasm is one of the most powerful engines of success. When you do a thing, do it with all your might. Put your whole soul in it. Stamp it with your own personality. Be active, be energetic, be enthusiastic and faithful, and you will accomplish your object. Nothing was ever achieved without enthusiasm.

—Ralph Waldo Emerson

Success is how high you bounce when you hit bottom.
—George Patton

If you don't like people, you will not know them, you will not know what scares them, inspires them, motivates them.

—Bo Schembechler

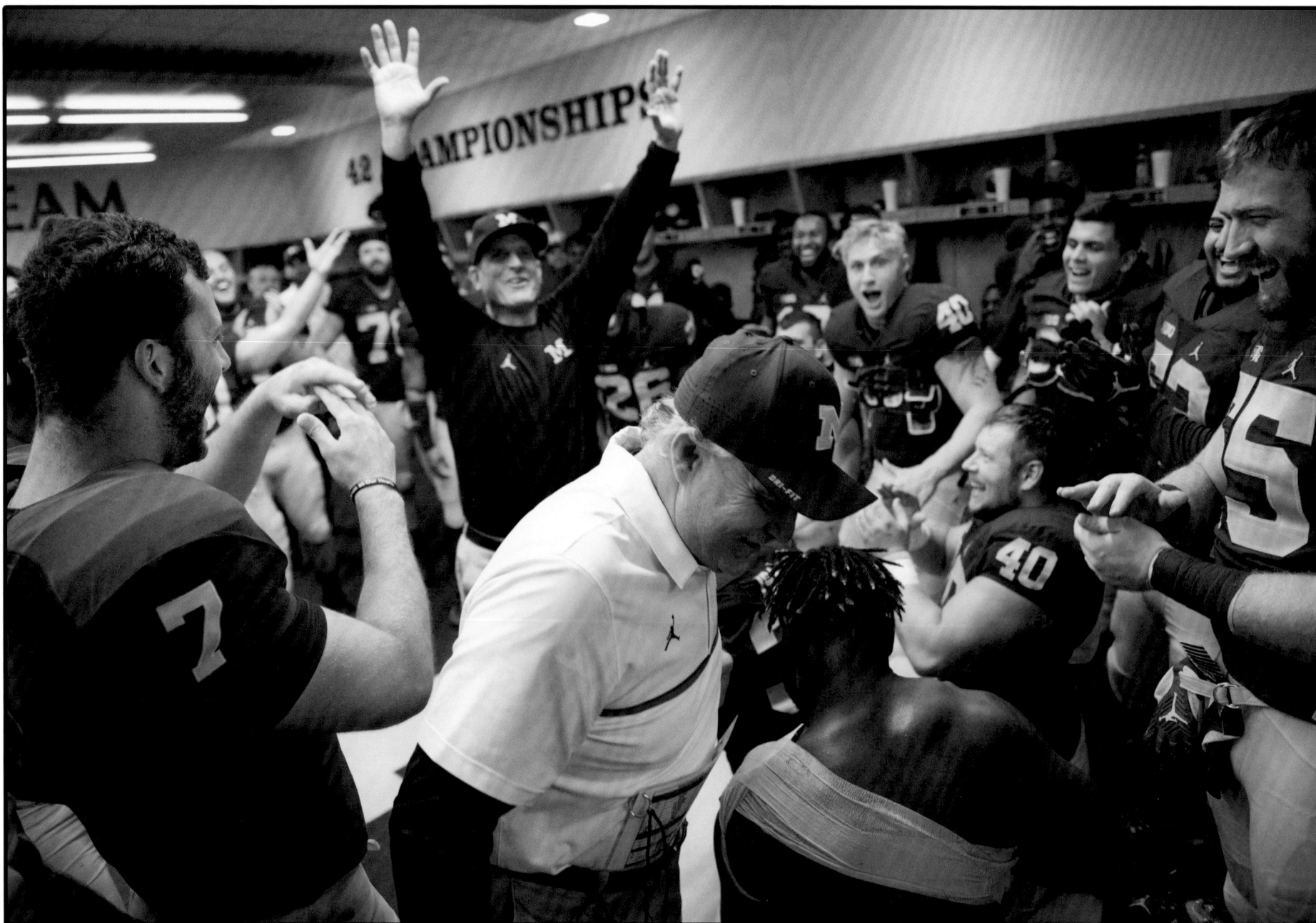

People are always blaming their circumstances for what they are.
I don't believe in circumstances. The people who get on in this world are the people who get up
and look for the circumstances they want, and if they don't find them they make them.

—George Bernard Shaw

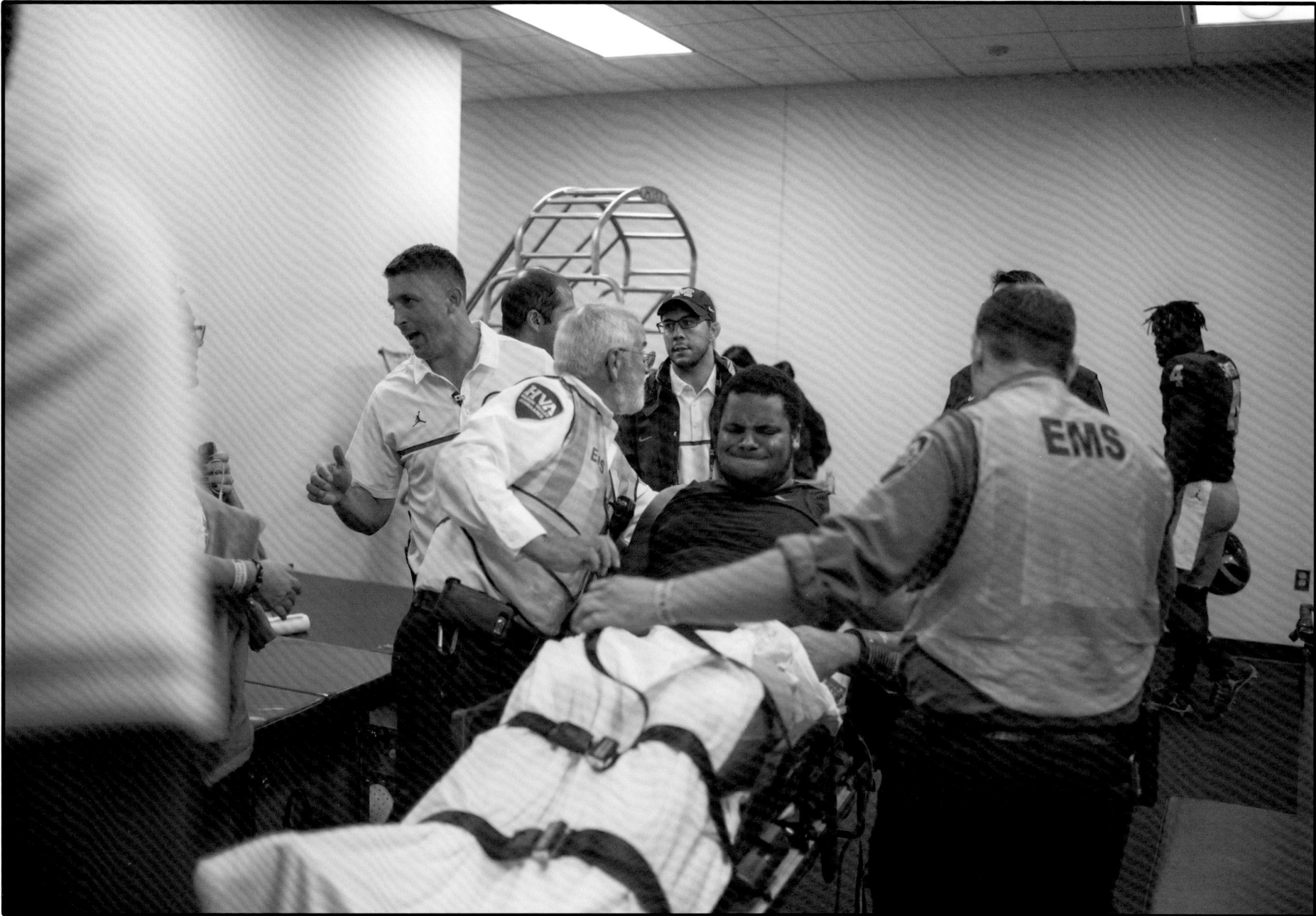

If no one is laughing at your dreams, you have not set your goals high enough.
—John Harbaugh

148   True loyalty is that quality of service that grows under adversity and expands in defeat. Any street urchin can shout applause in victory, but it takes character to stand fast in defeat. One is noise—the other—loyalty.

—Fielding Yost

Your children will have a lot of coaches but they have only one father.
Allow their coaches to coach and you be a supportive father.
—Jack Elway

Never let fundamentals and building skills take a back seat to game planning.
Game plans win games. Fundamentals win championships.
—Tom Crean

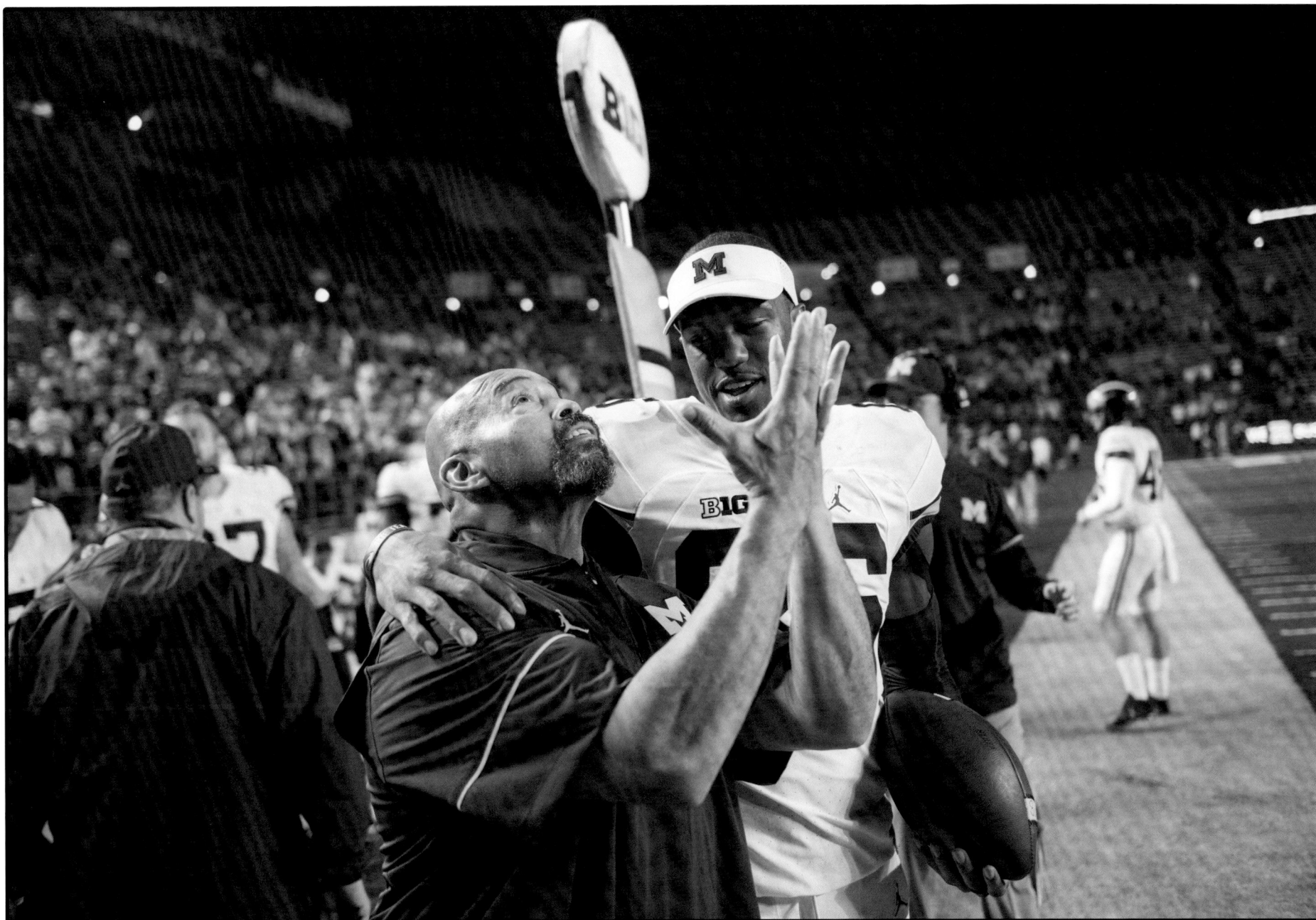

I figured this was the easy stuff and if we couldn't show up on time, looking right and acting right,
we weren't going to be able to do anything else.
—Bo Schembechler

Nothing good happens after midnight and when you get home I'll be waiting with milk and cookies.
—Jackie Harbaugh

I firmly believe that any man's finest hour, the greatest fulfillment of all that he holds dear, is that moment when he   161
has worked his heart out in a good cause and lies exhausted on the field of battle—victorious.
—Vince Lombardi

A good plan enthusiastically executed today is better than a perfect plan executed next week.
—George Patton

You never think about what life is going to be like five years down the road or ten. You just go through the day and try to make good decisions. Sometimes you do, sometimes you don't. You just hope this day is a good day.
—Jack Harbaugh

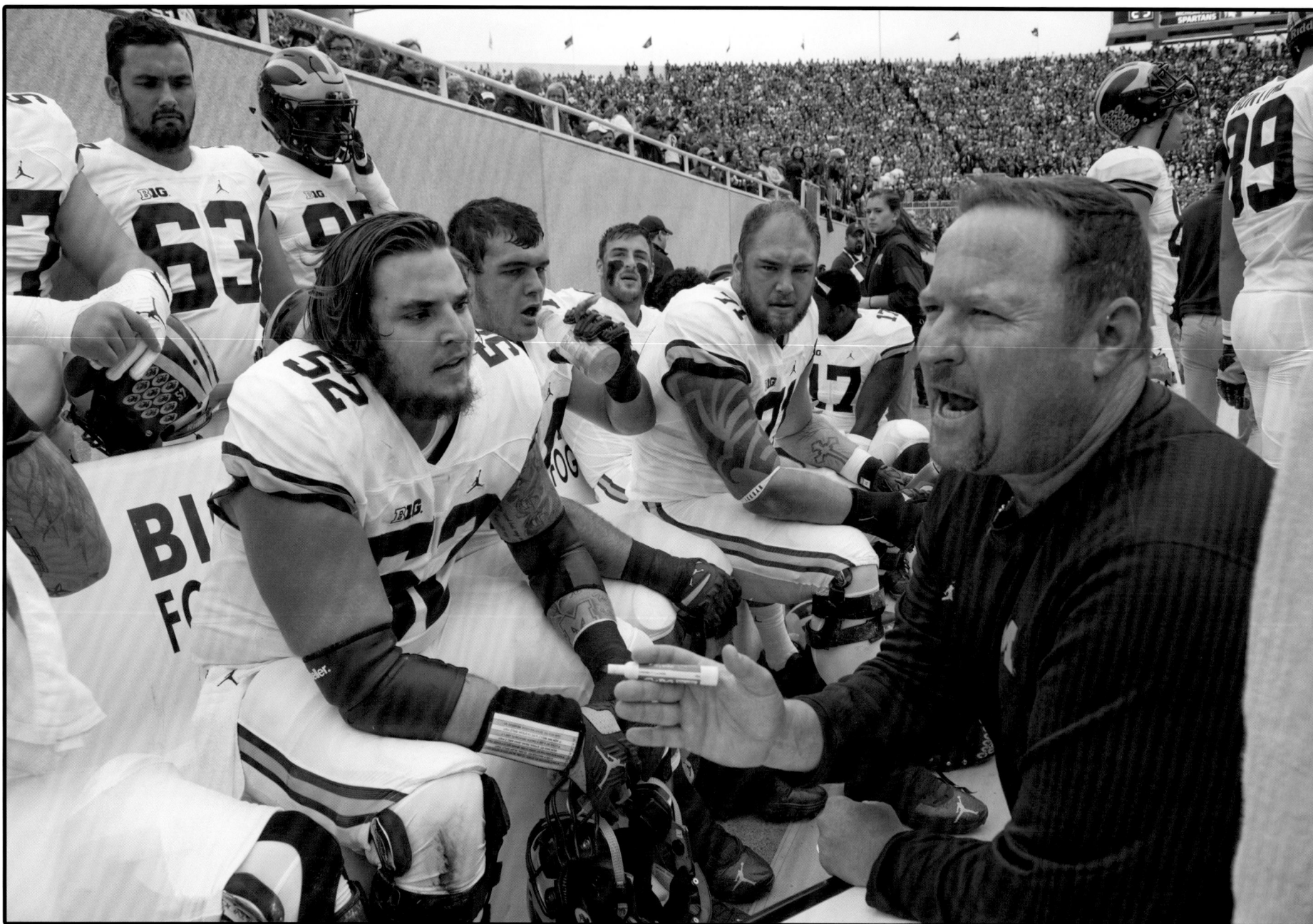

172

My soul is happy wherever my body takes me.
—Sarah Harbaugh

There are two groups of people in the world, those who work and those who take credit;
try to be in the first group, it is less crowded.
—Indira Gandhi

176   It is not the critic who counts; not the man who points out how the strong man stumbles, or where the doer of deeds could have done them better. The credit belongs to the man who is actually in the arena, whose face is marred by dust and sweat and blood; who strives valiantly; who errs, who comes short again and again, because there is no effort without error and shortcoming; but who does actually strive to do the deeds; who knows great enthusiasms,

the great devotions; who spends himself in a worthy cause; who at the best knows in the end the triumph of high achievement, and who at the worst, if he fails, at least fails while daring greatly, so that his place shall never be with those cold and timid souls who neither know victory nor defeat.

—Theodore Roosevelt

It ain't hard being a football player if you are a football player.
—Jim Harbaugh

You are getting better or you are getting worse. You never stay the same.
—Bo Schembechler

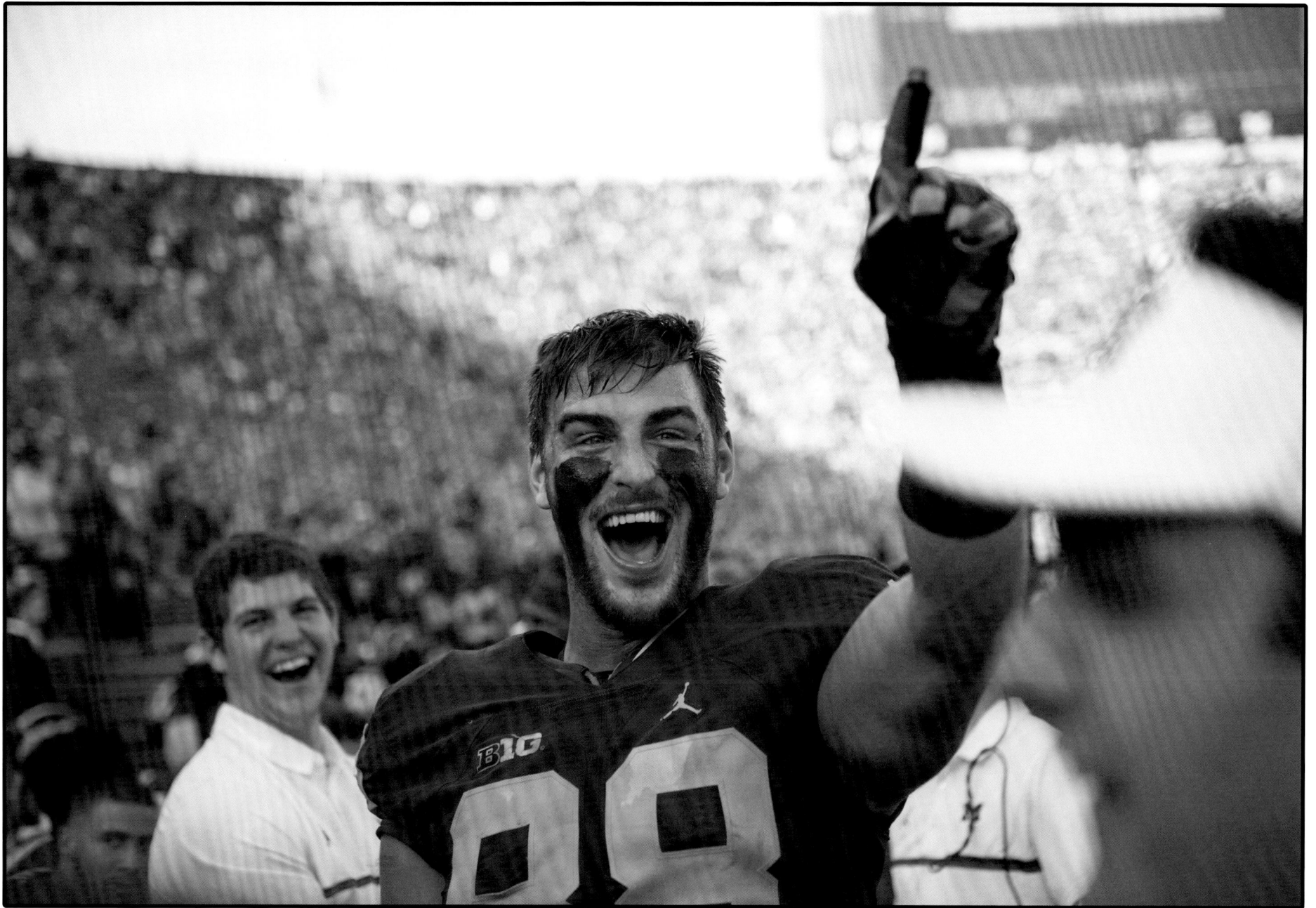

If I'm honest with you, you will not like me for a day or two, but if I lie to you, you'll hate me forever.
—Joe Maddon

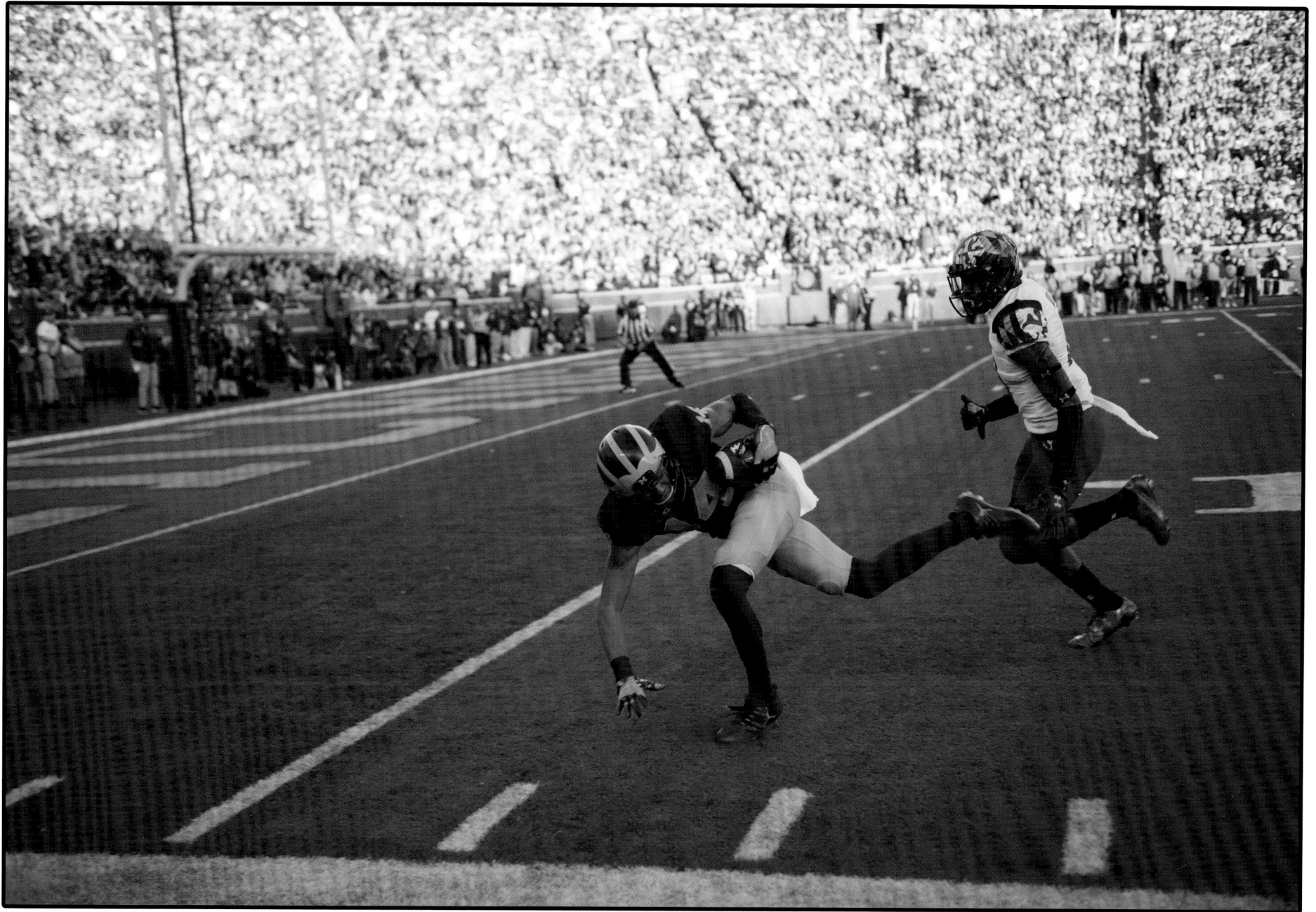

I never take vacations, I never get sick, I don't celebrate any major holidays,
I am a "Jack Hammer".
—Dwight K. Schrute

183

Don't tell me how rough the water or how rocky the shore just bring the ship in.
—Steve Stone

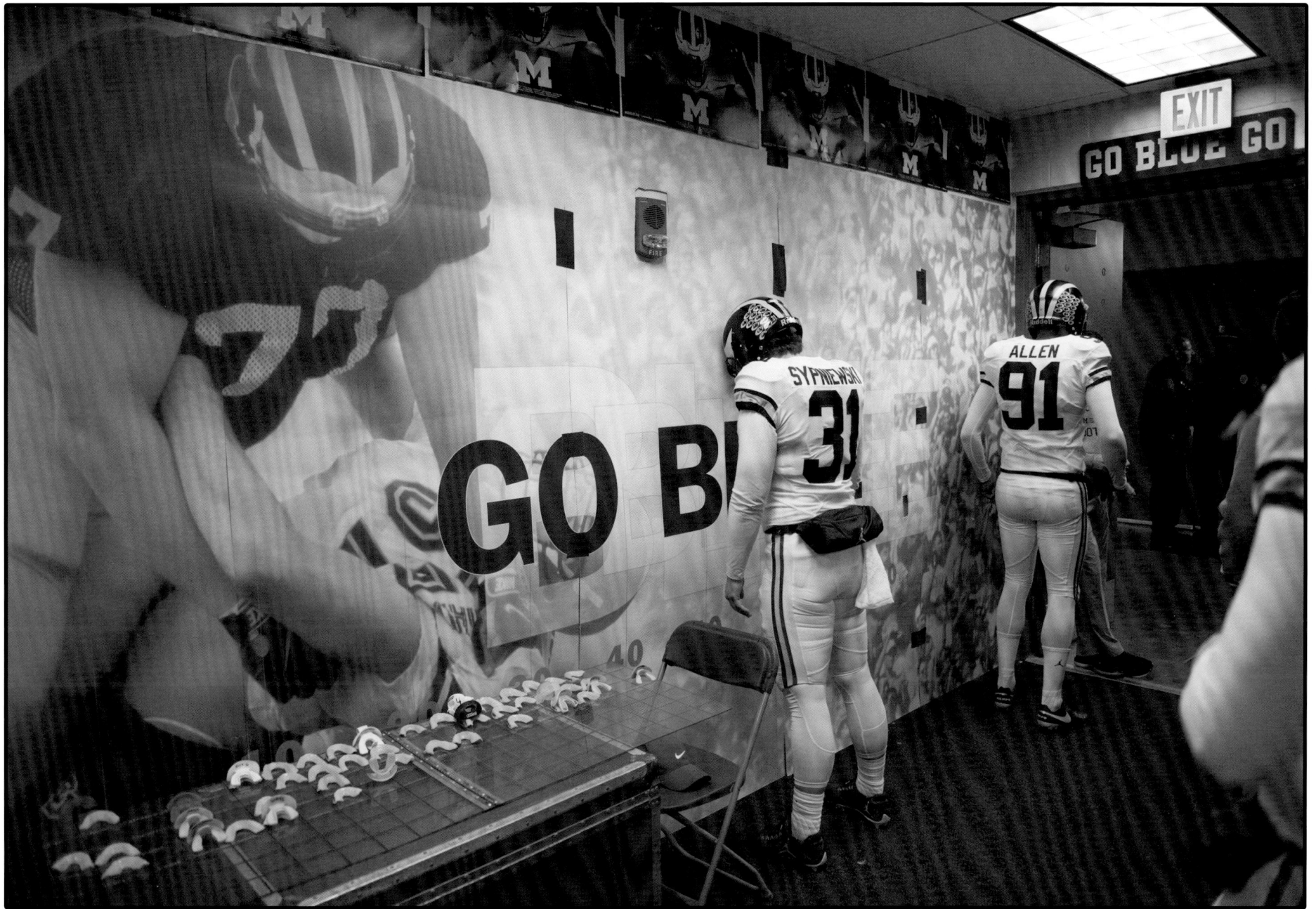

There's no family in America that celebrates victory better than the Harbaughs.
You'll never hear more laughter, more storytelling or more embellishment.
—Jack Harbaugh

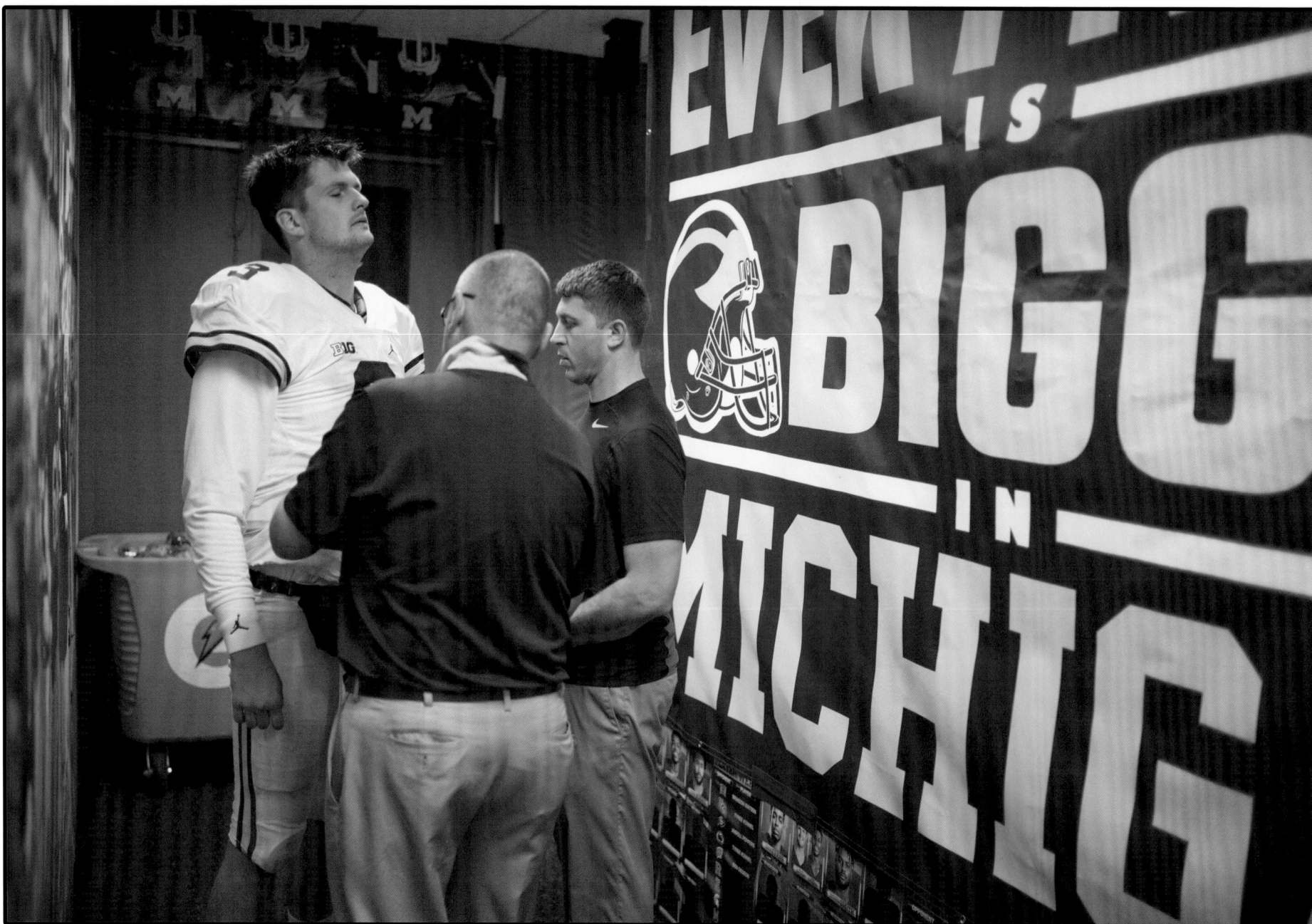

I shall pass through this world but once. Any good therefore that I can do or any kindness that I can show to any human being, let me do it now. Let me not defer or neglect it, for I shall not pass this way again.

—Stephen Grellet, through Joani Crean

Have you ever heard of someone who has played four years of football and said, "I wish I hadn't played"? It isn't said! But I have heard those who have said, "I wish I had played football."
—John Harbaugh

You must be unselfish and accept the role that helps your team win.
—Tom Crean

Be yourself. Everyone else is taken.
—Oscar Wilde

My greatest achievement was my ability to be able to convince my wife to marry me.
—Winston Churchill

210   Not making a decision is the worst thing you can do. So long as you feel you made the right decision based on the information you had at the time, there's no need to fret about it. If it fails, you'll know what to do the next time.

—Bo Schembechler

We are competing every day with everything and everybody, but most importantly, with ourselves.
—John Harbaugh

In traveling our great country, I have found our country's greatness lies within good,
proud people who possess faith, hope and love for family.
—Jim Harbaugh

Success consists of going from failure to failure without loss of enthusiasm.
—Winston Churchill

Do you want to be a successful football coach?
Have a love and passion for the game • Outwork your competition • Marry wisely
—Doyt Perry

It isn't what it is, it is what you have made it.

—Judge Judy

232   There are 5 things that I won't do for money. I won't kill for it. I won't marry for it. I won't lie, cheat or steal for it. Outside of that, I'm open to just about anything, especially working for it.
—Jim Harbaugh

What lies behind you and what lies in front of you, pales in comparison to what lies inside of you.
—Ralph Waldo Emerson

The Team, The Team, The Team
No man is more important than the team; no player, no coach,
The Team, The Team, The Team
We're going to believe in each other

We're not going to criticize each other. We're not going to talk about each other.
We're going to encourage each other.
And if we do that, when the season ends, we will be the Big Ten Champions.
—Bo Schembechler

You remember driving your kids to little league and they're talking about making the team and you're encouraging them. Forty years later, we're having the same conversation, only now it's about the Ravens-Steelers or Michigan-Ohio State.
—Jack Harbaugh

248 Be there…care…and put your children first in your life. When you are given the awesome responsibility of being a father that is the most important responsibility you will ever have! God wants us to have a loving relationship with our kids and help them grow…just like God's relationship with us.

—John Harbaugh

To win by cheating, is not winning.
—Bo Schembechler

Morale is to the physical as the #3 is to #1. Attitude is 3 times greater than your physical ability.
—Napoleon Bonaparte, through Bo Schembechler

No matter our loss, no matter our hardship, this family will never "stand down."
—Frank Reagan

A man can be destroyed, but not defeated.
—Ernest Hemingway

Success is not final, failure is not final; it is the courage to continue that counts.
—Winston Churchill

Football at Michigan is a meritocracy; a system in which the talented are chosen
and moved ahead on the basis of daily improvement.
—Jim Harbaugh

Ability is God given, prowess is earned.
—John Harbaugh

We few, we happy few. We band of brothers, for he today that sheds his blood with me shall be my brother.
—William Shakespeare

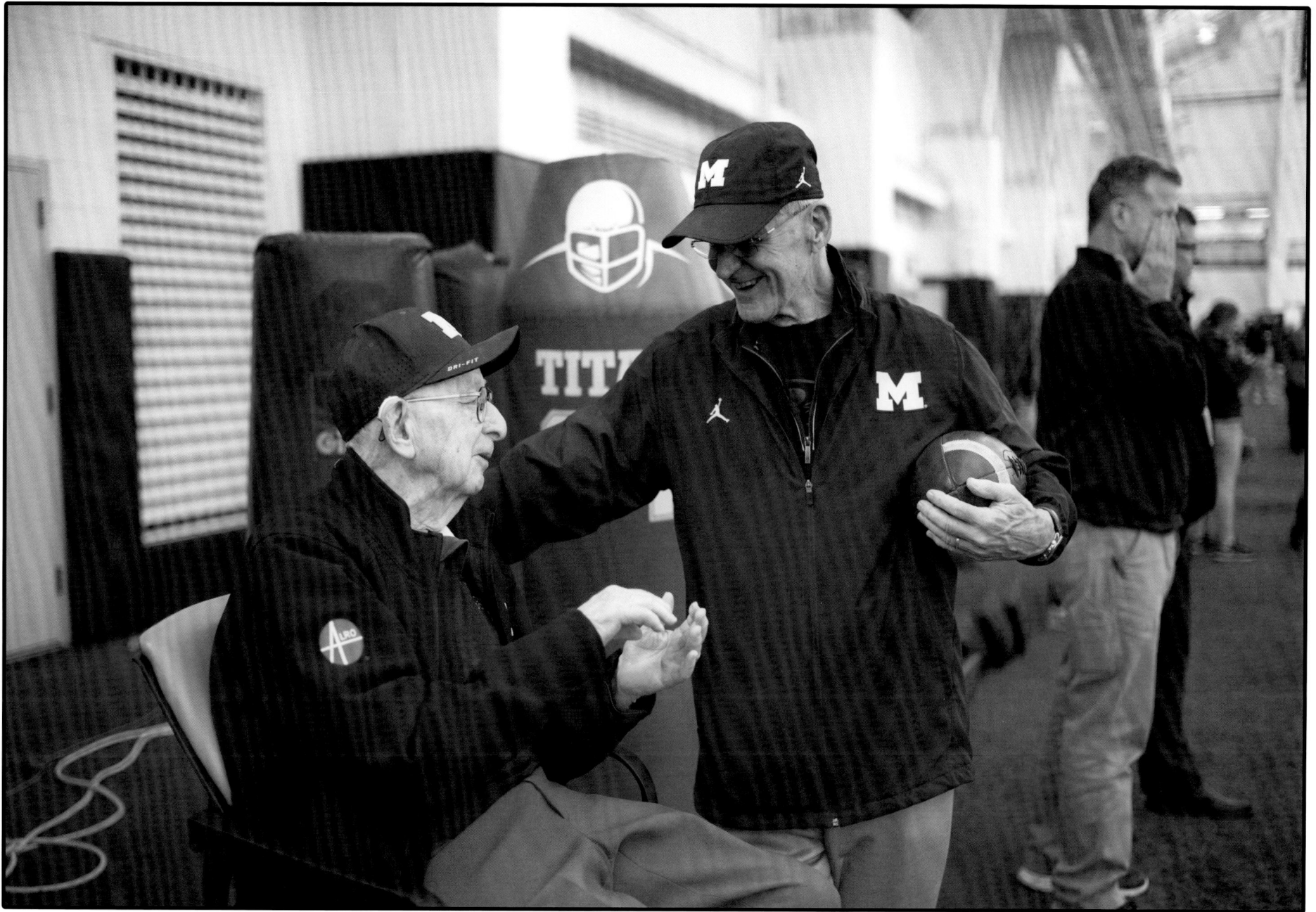

To laugh often and much; to win the respect of intelligent people and the affection of children, to leave the world a better place, to know even one life has breathed easier because you have lived, this is to have succeeded.
—Ralph Waldo Emerson

I'm not into "if this" or "if that" type of scenarios. If worms had machine guns, then birds wouldn't mess with them.
—Jim Harbaugh

Football games aren't won, they are lost.
—Fielding Yost

You have enemies?
Good! That means you've stood up for something, sometime in your life.
—Winston Churchill

Every day is a fistfight. Every day you must be prepared to fight and to win.
—John Harbaugh

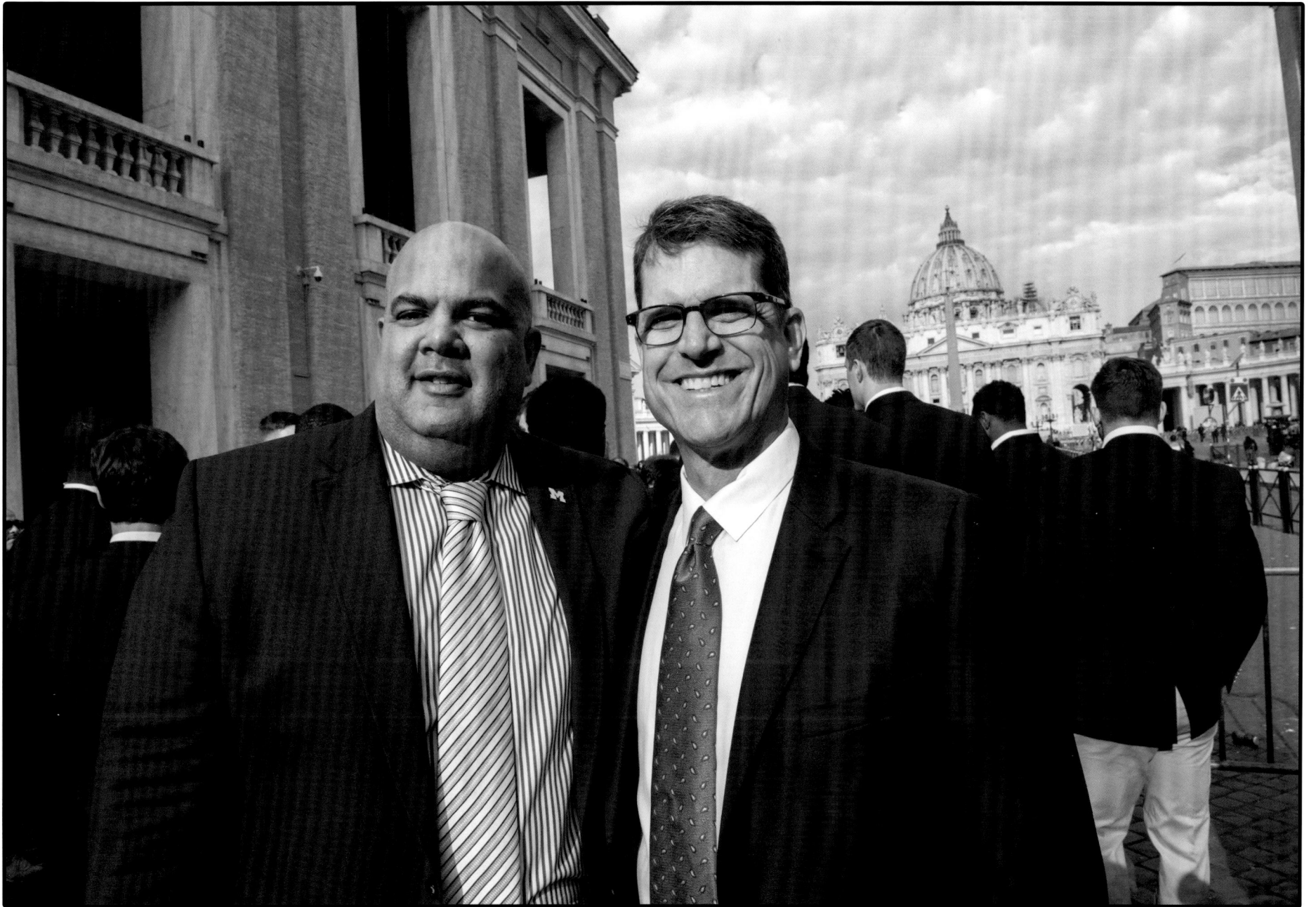

A father's legacy to his son.
He played catch with him. He took him to games. He believed in him.
—Bob Feller

There are three kinds of people in the world.
Ones that watch things happen. • Ones that make things happen. • Ones that wonder what happened.
—Anonymous

I think everyone should go to college and get a degree and then spend six months as a bartender and six months as a cab driver. Then they would really be educated.
—Al McGuire

We do something very special every day in football, a dirty four letter word. WORK
—Jim Harbaugh

Live in a state of grace. Put your trust in the Lord. Be not afraid.
—Merle Feuerborn

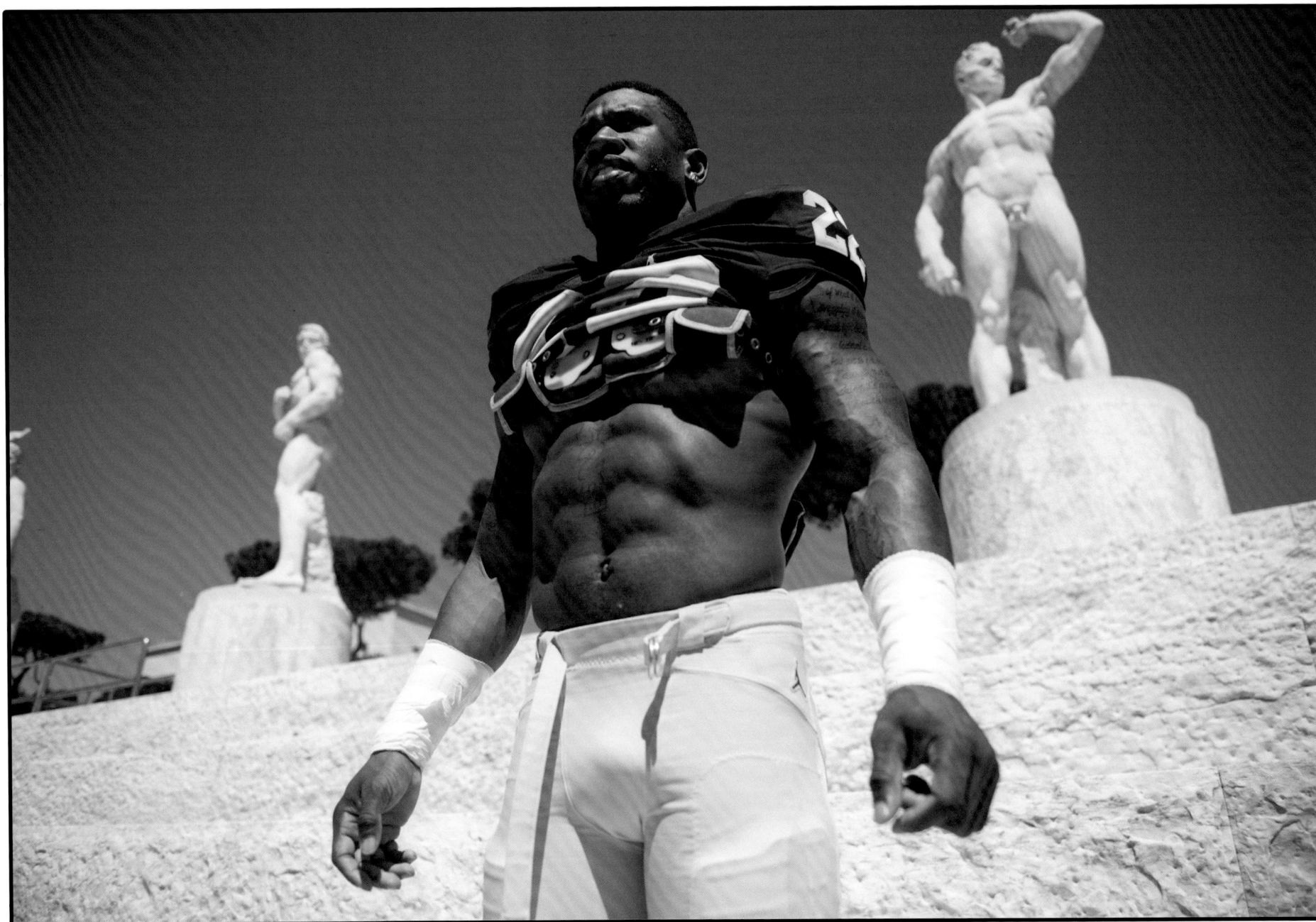

310

Lead like Truman, don't tap dance like Fred Astaire.

—Jim Harbaugh

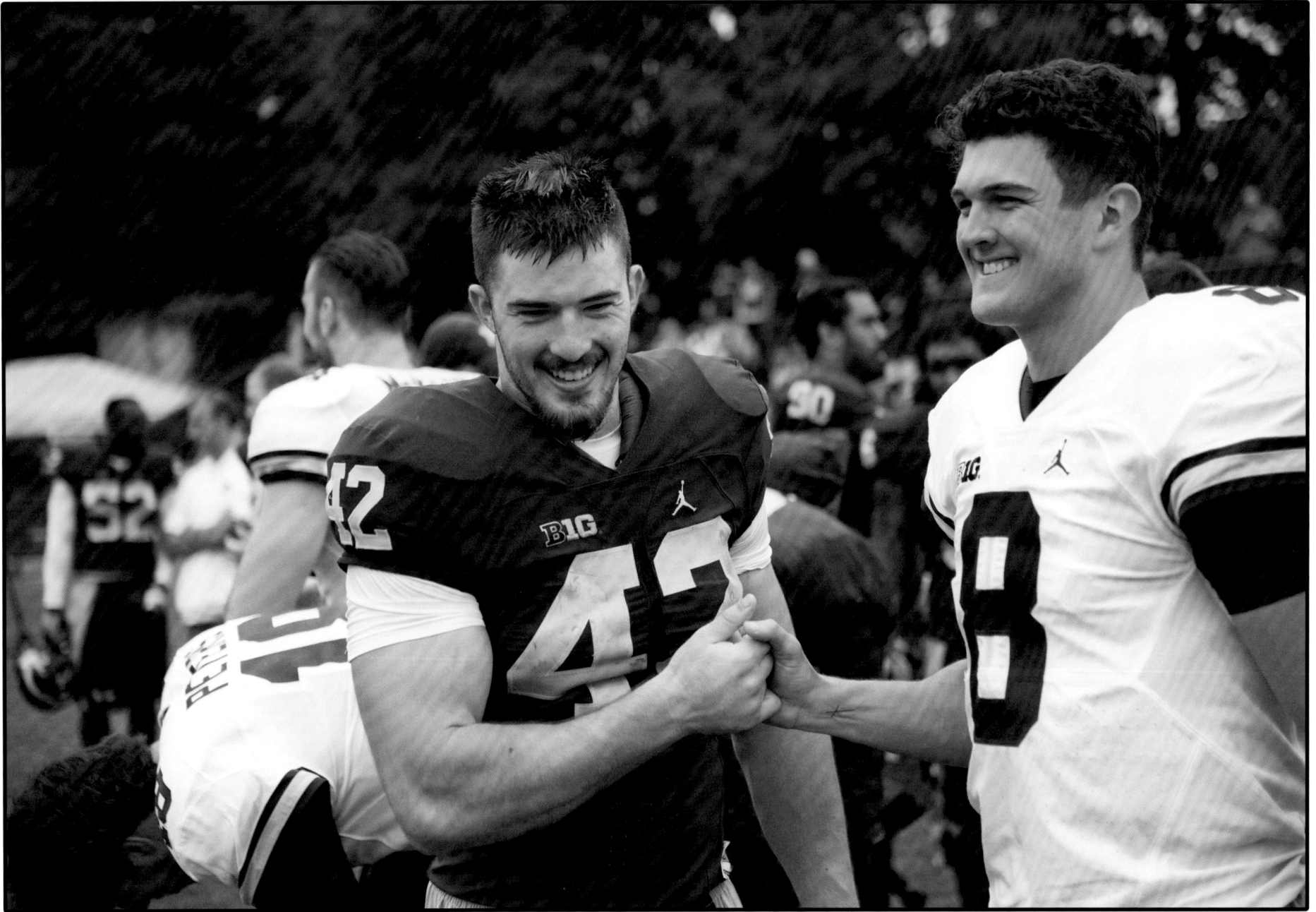

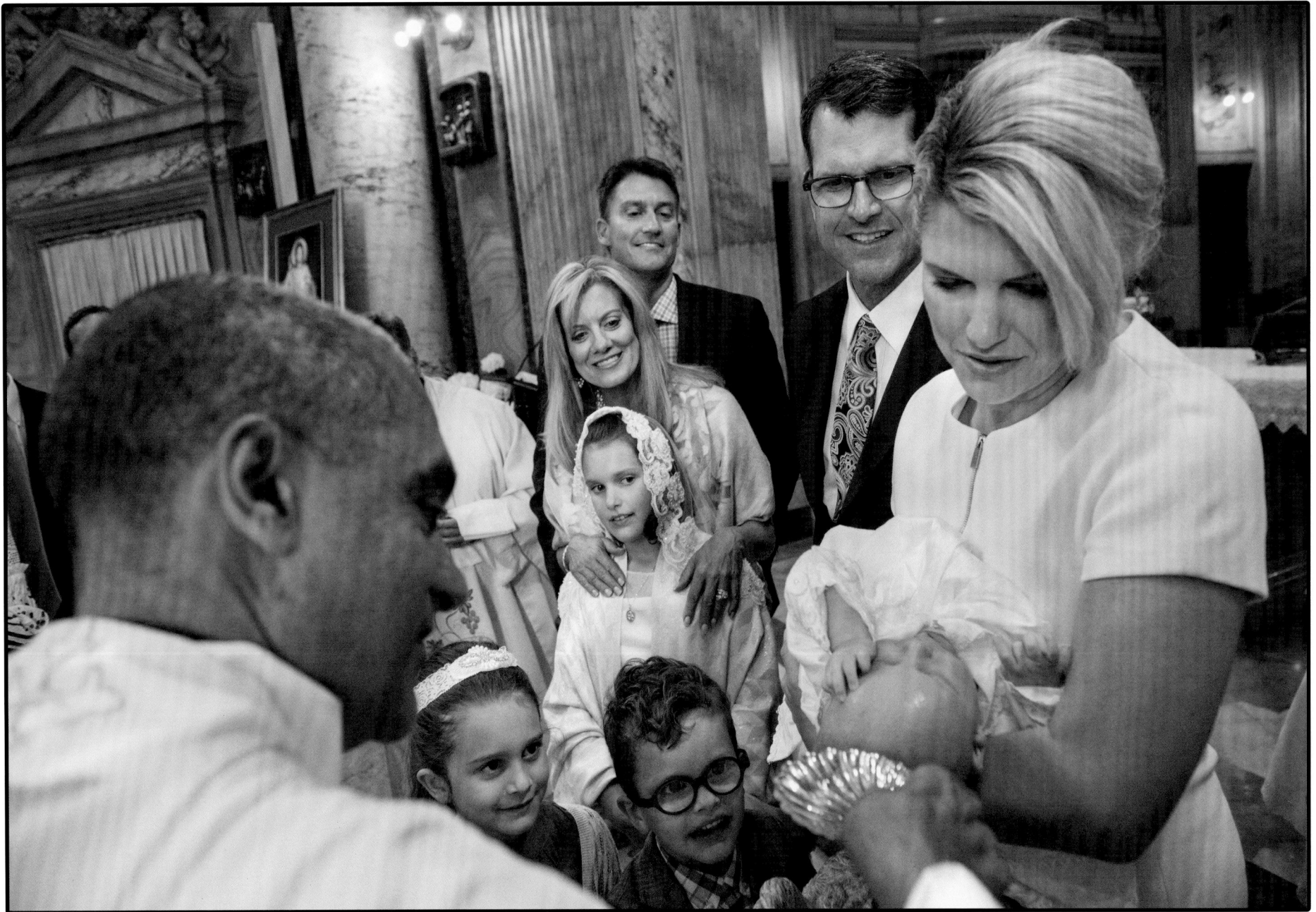

316   We think sometimes that poverty is only being hungry, naked and homeless. The poverty of being unwanted,
unloved and uncared for is the greatest poverty. We must start in our own homes to remedy this kind of poverty.
—Mother Teresa

318 My heart is so full at this moment, I fear I could say little else. But do let me reiterate the Spirit of Michigan. It is based on a deathless loyalty to Michigan and all her ways. An enthusiasm that makes it second nature for Michigan Men to spread the gospel of their university to the world's distant outposts. And a conviction that nowhere, is there a better university, in any way, than this Michigan of ours.

—Fielding Yost, In Retirement Address

BIOGRAPHIES

AUTHORS

Jim Harbaugh was named the 20th coach in Michigan football history on Dec. 30, 2014, becoming the sixth former Michigan football player to lead college football's all-time winningest program. Harbaugh joins Fielding Yost as one of two coaches in Michigan history to earn back-to-back seasons of double digit victories to begin their head coaching tenure at Michigan. Harbaugh arrived in Ann Arbor after an impressive four-year run in the NFL with the San Francisco 49ers. He led the franchise to the NFC championship game in each of his first three seasons, winning the George Halas Trophy as NFC Champions in 2012.

Prior to making the jump to the 49ers, Harbaugh established himself as a leader at the college level. At Stanford, the Cardinal improved in each of his four seasons. Harbaugh finished his tenure at Stanford with a 29–21 overall record and 21–15 mark in the Pac-10 Conference. His 2010 squad posted a 12–1 overall record (8–1 Pac-10) and was selected for a BCS bowl game, defeating Virginia Tech, 40–12, in the FedEx Orange Bowl. The Cardinal finished the 2010 season ranked fifth in the national polls, and Harbaugh was awarded the Woody Hayes Award as the nation's top coach by the Touchdown Club of Columbus.

In his first head coaching experience, Harbaugh led the University of San Diego to a 29–6 record and back-to-back Pioneer Football League championships during his three seasons (2004–06). Harbaugh spent the 2002 and 2003 NFL seasons as the quarterbacks coach with the Oakland Raiders. He helped the organization reach Super Bowl XXXVII after winning the AFC Western Division title. Harbaugh began preparing for a coaching career during his professional playing days. He spent eight years as an NCAA-certified unpaid assistant coach for his father, Jack, at Western Kentucky (1994–2001). He worked as an offensive consultant and recruited for the Hilltoppers during that time, helping his father's team capture the 2002 Division I-AA national championship.

Harbaugh played for five organizations during his 15-year NFL career (1987–2001). He completed 2,305-of-3,918 passes for 26,288 yards and 129 touchdowns in 177 games with 140 career starts. He was named the AFC Offensive Player of the Year, the NFL Comeback Player of the Year and was a Pro Bowl selection after leading the Indianapolis Colts to the AFC Championship Game in 1995.

Playing for the University of Michigan under Bo Schembechler, Harbaugh led the nation in pass efficiency in 1985 and finished as the runner-up in 1986. His career pass efficiency rating was the NCAA's top mark for more than 12 years. Harbaugh won the Chicago Tribune Big Ten Most Valuable Player award, earned first-team All-America honors and finished third in Heisman Trophy balloting following the 1986 season. He completed 387-of-620 passes for 5,449 yards and 31 touchdowns at Michigan. Harbaugh led the Wolverines to a 21–3–1 record as a full-time starter during his final two seasons.

Harbaugh and his wife, Sarah, have two daughters, Addison and Katherine, and two sons, Jack and John. He also has three children, Jay, James Jr., and Grace. Harbaugh is the son of Jack and Jackie Harbaugh. Jack was an assistant coach at Michigan from 1973–79. Harbaugh's brother, John, is head coach of the Baltimore Ravens and Harbaugh's sister, Joani, is married to collegiate basketball coach Tom Crean.

David Turnley is a winner of the Pulitzer Prize for Photography and is considered one of the best documentary photographers in the world. David was a finalist for the Pulitzer Prize four additional times.

David won the Pulitzer Prize for his coverage of the Revolutions in Eastern Europe and Tiananmen Square in China. He was awarded the prestigious Robert Capa Gold Medal for Courage. This work was published in two books: In Times Of War and Peace and Beijing Spring.

David's photograph from the Gulf War in Iraq is considered one of the most iconic in the history of photography. He won the World Press Picture of the Year. David also won the World Press Picture of the Year for his photograph in Armenia following a devastating earthquake.

David's work in South Africa and with Nelson Mandela earned international recognition and was published in two books: Why Are They Weeping: South Africans Under Apartheid and Mandela: Struggle And Triumph. He was awarded the Leica Oskar Barnack Award and the University of Missouri Canon Essay Award.

As the Soviet Union was collapsing, David traveled across 13 Republics to photograph and write a book The Russian Heart.

David was smuggled in a truck tire inner tube across the Tigres, and Euphrates Rivers, by Kurdish Guerillas, into Northern Iraq, to cover the second Iraq War. He wrote and photographed a book titled Baghdad Blues.

David was awarded the Overseas Press Club Olivier Rebbot award for his work documenting the plight of refugees in the war in Bosnia and that same year photographed the war in Afghanistan.

On 9/11, David went into the rubble with firemen, after having to dive into a building to avoid being crushed by falling debris, as he photographed the collapse of the World Trade Center.

David has Directed three Documentary Films. In At Home and In Exile, David lived for three days with the Dalai Lama in India. In La Tropical, he spent a summer filming a dance hall on the edge of Havana where the best Cuban dancers have always gone to dance to the best Cuban musicians. In Shenandoah, David filmed a tough coal-mining town in Pennsylvania, blown apart when four star white football players beat to death an undocumented Mexican immigrant. Shenandoah won Best Film from the LA New Filmmakers and David was honored with the Award for Best Director.

David was raised in Fort Wayne, Indiana where he grew up playing football. He and his twin brother Peter discovered photography at 17. They spent two years documenting an inner city street in their industrial hometown and published a book titled McClellan Street.

CBS 60 Minutes produced a profile of the Turnley brothers titled "Double Exposure" calling them two of the great photographers of our time.

David has a BA in French Literature from the University of Michigan. He has studied at the Sorbonne in Paris, and at Harvard on a Neiman Fellowship. He has won Honorary Doctorates from the New School for Social Research in New York City and St. Francis College in Indiana.

In 2015 David received tenure as an Associate Professor at The University of Michigan, his alma mater, teaching Documentary Photography.

In that same year he earned the trust of Coach Jim Harbaugh and the honor to document the Michigan Football Team with unprecedented access. Together Coach Harbaugh and David have co-authored *Enthusiasm Unknown To Mankind*, an exquisite coffee table book with some 300 museum quality black and white photographs. *Rise Again*, is the second volume in the Enthusiasm Unknown to Mankind series.

David is married to Rachel, an accomplished contemporary ballet dancer. He has two children, Charlie, 23, and Dawson, 5.

— AUTHORS —

PLAYERS · KENNETH ALLEN · DEVIN ASIASI · JOE BENEDUCCI · BEN BRADEN · BEN BREDESON · AUSTIN BRENNER · IAN BUNTING DEVIN BUSH · PETER BUSH · JUWANN BUSHELL-BEATTY · JAKE BUTT · TACO CHARLTON · CAMARON CHEESEMAN · JEHU CHESSON BRIAN CHU · JEREMY CLARK · TYLER COCHRAN · MASON COLE · KEKOA CRAWFORD · ANTHONY DALIMONTE · AMARA DARBOH KINGSTON DAVIS · DAVID DAWSON · SPENCER DICKOW · DANE DROBOCKY · JACK DUNAWAY · MICHAEL DWUMFOUR CONNER EDMONDS · NICK EUBANKS · CHRIS EVANS · KENNETH FERRIS · JOSEPH FILES · JAMES FOUG · GREG FROELICH NOAH FURBUSH · RASHAN GARY · BEN GEDEON · ZACH GENTRY · DEVIN GIL · JORDAN GLASGOW · RYAN GLASGOW MATTHEW GODIN · LOUIS GRODMAN · DRAKE HARRIS · WILL HART · BOBBY HENDERSON · JOE HEWLETT · KARAN HIGDON DELANO HILL · KHALID HILL · LAVERT HILL · MICHAEL HIRSCH · KHALEKE HUDSON · MAURICE HURST · TY ISAAC MICHAEL JOCZ · DRAKE JOHNSON · NATE JOHNSON · RON JOHNSON · SHELTON JOHNSON · DAN JOKISCH · REUBEN JONES KYLE KALIS · ALEX KAMINSKI · ANTHONY KAY · CARLO KEMP · TYREE KINNEL · TAYLOR KRUPP · PATRICK KUGLER JOURDAN LEWIS · DAVID LONG · ERIK MAGNUSON · SALIM MAKKI · ALEX MALZONE · LAWRENCE MARSHALL · JAKE MARTIN ELYSEE MBEM-BOSSE · MIKE MCCRAY · EDDIE MCDOOM · SEAN MCKEON · JOSH METELLUS · GARRETT MILLER · MATT MITCHELL BRYAN MONE · GARRETT MOORES · SHANE MORRIS · CARL MYERS · GRANT NEWSOME · QUINN NORDIN · JOHN O'KORN JAMESON OFFERDAHL · MICHAEL ONWENU · AJ PEARSON · JABRILL PEPPERS · GRANT PERRY · BRANDON PETERS BEN PLISKA · HENRY POGGI · CHEYENN ROBERTSON · ANDREW ROBINSON · GREG ROBINSON · JON RUNYAN · NATE SCHOENLE MICHAEL SESSA · WYATT SHALLMAN · KENNETH SLOSS · DE'VEON SMITH · SIMEON SMITH · STEPHEN SPANELLIS WILTON SPEIGHT · CHANNING STRIBLING · SCOTT SYPNIEWSKI · DYMONTE THOMAS · RYAN TICE · JOSH UCHE NOLAN ULIZIO ANDREW VASTARDIS · NICK VOLK · KAREEM WALKER · JACK WANGLER · JARED WANGLER · KEITH WASHINGTON BRANDON WATSON · MAURICE WAYS · JACOB WEST · TYRONE WHEATLEY · BRENDAN WHITE · TRU WILSON · CHASE WINOVICH CHRIS WORMLEY · MICHAEL WROBLEWSKI · SPRING · TARICK BLACK · JARED CHAR · TRAVIS DANTZER · JA'RAYMOND HALL WILLIAM HOLTON · DONOVAN JETER · BRADFORD JONES · NICHOLAS KELLS · JAYLEN KELLY-POWELL · ERIC KIM · JOHN LUBY COREY MALONE-HATCHER · BEN MASON · DONOVAN PEOPLES-JONES · CESAR RUIZ · KYLE SEYCHEL · BENJAMIN ST-JUSTE AMBRY THOMAS · JOSH WILK · J'MARICK WOODS

COACHES · JIM HARBAUGH · DON BROWN · TIM DREVNO · JEDD FISCH · JAY HARBAUGH · GREG MATTISON · CHRIS PARTRIDGE BRIAN SMITH · TYRONE WHEATLEY · MIKE ZORDICH · GREG FREY · PEP HAMILTON · GRADUATE ASSISTANTS/ANALYSTS JIMMIE DOUGHERTY · ANTONIO RICHARDS · MICHAEL SWITZER · AL NETTER · DREW TERRELL · RYAN NEHLEN · DAVE ADOLPH DEVIN BUSH · RICK FINOTTI · JOE HASTINGS · TYLER BROWN · BO DEVER · SCOTT TURNER · KEVIN LEMPA · MIKE BROWN JORDAN KOVACS · PERFORMANCE · FERGUS CONNOLLY · OPERATIONS · JIM MINICK · AL ADES · TONY DEFEO ZACH EISENDRATH · JON FALK J.T. ROGAN · JOHN ROTCHE · TYRAN STEWARD · KELLY KING · SCOTT GOLDSCHMIDT EQUIPMENT · GARY HAZELITTSONNY ANDERSON · BRETT MCGINNESS · KORI REBLIN ATHLETIC MEDICINE · DAVE GRANITO PHIL JOHNSON · JASON WILLIAMS · GRIFFIN HADDAD · LENNY NAVITSKIS · VAHAN AGBABIAN · ASHEESH BEDI · BRUCE MILLER AMY MILLER · KYLEE PHILLIPS · RECRUITING · SEAN MAGEE · TONY TUIOTI · AARON BILLS · TONY BINKER · CHRIS BRYANT GWEN BUSH · ALBERT KARSCHNIA · COOPER PATANGA · ANTONIO POOLE · TY ROGERS · ELIJAH SANDWEISS · ADAM SCHRACK STRENGTH AND CONDITIONING · KEVIN TOLBERT · NATE BARRY · MARK NAYLOR · JIM PLOCKI · COREY TWINE · VIDEO PHIL BROMLEY · KEVIN UNDEEN · DENNIS BLANCHARD · CHRIS FOX · MIKE BAKER · SCHEMBECHLER HALL · BIFF BUNTEN BRIAN BURD · KYLE DEKEYSER · MICHELLE GUIDRY-PAN · JEFF PIPKINS · ACADEMICS · STEVE CONNELLY · CLAIBORNE GREEN SARAH RECHNITZER · SHARI ACHO · COMMUNICATIONS · DAVE ABLAUF · CHAD SHEPARD ADMINISTRATION · WARDE MANUEL · DOUG GNODTKE

2016 STUDENT ASSISTANTS · EVENTS · JASON ANGUS · RACHEL COLYER · THEO ENDRESEN DIANTE HARRIS · HALLEY HARRIS · LIAM HOULIHAN · MIA HUTCHINSON · AMARIS NICKERSON OSHRI OLSBERG · MACKENZIE PALLANTE · JONATHON PERRY · MARK RAMIREZ · RACHEL REA MICHAEL SCHWARTZ · NELL SHULDINER · NICOLE SIGMON · SHELBY SIMS · ABBEY ZACHARIAS EQUIPMENT/MANAGERS · MAX BERNSTEIN · QUENTIN BUCKLEY · MATT CURTIS · BEN DUNCAN BENNETT FALISKI · WILL HENNESSY · RAMI KADOUH · SAM KHYM · JACOB KOSTNER · PATRICK LELICH ALEC LONDAL · ZACH MUIR · CAREY NEFF · EVAN ROSEN · QUENTIN TEDESCO · SCHAEFER THELEN CLAYTON TURNER · AARON VAN HORN · TRISTIN WIEGERS · TYLER WINTERICH · CARL FARAON BEN WRIGHT · CJ MCGORISK · JACK CRONYN · MITCH SCHWOCHO · ANDREW COLEMAN · OPERATIONS ERIN CRONYN · LINA FRY · NIKKI PATEL · TANNER TRUSCOTT · PERFORMANCE SCIENCE SOPH BAUR-WAISBORD · ADAM BELCHER · DEVEN BHATT · CAROLINE BOWMAN · AVNEET CHADHA SCOTT FELDPAUSCH KATIE GIARMO · MADDIE HANSON · JAMIE OCKNER · MOLLY O'SULLIVAN · DANIEL ROSE EMMA SHEFFERT · · RECRUITING · KEITH ABDENOUR · CHAD ANTONELLI · GREGORY AUERBACH KALA COSTON · REON DAWSON · MIKAYLA DURANT · BRIAN GALVIN · EMILY HAYDEL · RILEY HOLDER LEON JOHNSON · JARED KOHLENBERG · CHYANNE LALDEE · BRANDEN LEVINE · CARISSA MARTIN JONAE MAXEY · TESS MORALES · SAM POPPER · SHANE REED · DANNIE ROGERS · CARLENA TOOMBS JAMIE WESTERMAN · RYAN WHITE · CAMERON WING · COMMUNICATIONS/SPORTS INFORMATION KATHARINE BOHLMANN · COURTNEY BOSTIC · KATIE CONKLIN · AMELIA GIRGENTI · SARAH HAMPTON OLIVIA PAUL · CALEB ROSENFELD · STRENGTH AND CONDITIONING · MATT DEHAVEN · LOGAN PRATT JOSH VERRAN · CONNOR WILLIAMS · VIDEO · BRYSON RHODES · BRENDAN SKINNER · SOHAM MISHRA WILLIAM MCCORMACK · ANDREW BENNETT-BELCH · BRIAN DIEFENBACH · ALEX BUGAJSKI MICHAEL BENEDETTO · JOSE ENRIGUE RIVERA COLLAZO · ANTHONY CANDIELLO · TIM MANN THEODORE FUNDRESON · ATHLETIC MEDICINE · ADAM OLSZEWSKI · EMILY AARON · ALICE JEONG JUSTIN BOCKHOLT · CYNDEY ROGERS · SHAYLYN O'KEEFE · ARIANA SENN · MALLORY GRABILL MOHAN DONG · KAILEY DANAHER · KAYLA NUGENT · JENNIE DRAZIN · BRIANNA KENNEDY · SAM SCHRODER